What Successful Teachers Do

Other titles by Mary C. Clement
Building the Best Faculty: Strategies for Hiring and Supporting New Teachers
First Time in the College Classroom: A Guide for Teaching Assistants, Instructors, and New Professors at All Colleges and Universities
First Time in the High School Classroom: Essential Guide for the New Teacher
Get a Teaching Job NOW: A Step-by-Step Guide
Retaining Effective Teachers: A Guide for Hiring, Induction, and Support
So You Want to Be a Teacher?
The Definitive Guide to Getting a Teaching Job: An Insider's Guide to Finding the Right Job, Writing the Perfect Resume, and Nailing the Interview

What Successful Teachers Do

A Dozen Things to Ensure Student Learning

Mary C. Clement

ROWMAN & LITTLEFIELD
Lanham • Boulder • New York • London

Published by Rowman & Littlefield
An imprint of The Rowman & Littlefield Publishing Group, Inc.
4501 Forbes Boulevard, Suite 200, Lanham, Maryland 20706
www.rowman.com

Unit A, Whitacre Mews, 26-34 Stannary Street, London SE11 4AB

Copyright © 2018 by Mary C. Clement

All rights reserved. No part of this book may be reproduced in any form or by any electronic or mechanical means, including information storage and retrieval systems, without written permission from the publisher, except by a reviewer who may quote passages in a review.

British Library Cataloguing in Publication Information Available

Library of Congress Cataloging-in-Publication Data Available

ISBN 978-1-4758-4349-1 (cloth : alk. paper)
ISBN 978-1-4758-4350-7 (pbk. : alk. paper)
ISBN 978-1-4758-4351-4 (electronic)

∞ ™ The paper used in this publication meets the minimum requirements of American National Standard for Information Sciences Permanence of Paper for Printed Library Materials, ANSI/NISO Z39.48-1992.

Printed in the United States of America

This book is dedicated to Bill and Cheri Clement, and to Gary and Wanda Palmer. Thank you for what you have done, and continue to do, to help my mother in Illinois. Because each of you cares for Mother, I have more time to work and write in Georgia. My deepest thanks for your thoughtfulness and kindness.

My thanks also go out to Tom Koerner, at Rowman & Littlefield Education. Tom is a great editor who has supported my writing for many years.

Contents

Preface: What Defines Success in Teaching?   ix
Introduction   xi

1. Prepare Personally and Professionally   1
2. Know Educational Psychology   13
3. Organize and Manage the Classroom   29
4. Plan for Teaching   45
5. Use Effective Methods and Strategies   59
6. Use Technology   73
7. Assess Student Work   85
8. Meet the Needs of All Students   101
9. Communicate with All Stakeholders   115
10. Manage Time and Stress   129
11. Grow as Professionals   141
12. Know Why They Teach   157

References   167
Index   171
About the Author   173

Preface

What Defines Success in Teaching?

When I was a high school teacher, I often defined success as getting to 3:20 on Friday afternoon. I definitely felt successful on the last day of the school year. What a feeling to know I had survived another year, seen a class of seniors graduate, and had ten glorious weeks of freedom ahead of me. Now, with almost forty years of teaching experience, I view success not so much as getting to the end of the week or year but more so in terms of the level of help and hope I have given students. My personal sense of efficacy—knowing that I can reach students and affect their lives for the better—probably fuels my sense of success. I am in the stage of my career where I want to share and maybe even inspire.

In the early 1990s, I was asked to give a motivational talk at an in-service teachers' program in Mt. Vernon, Illinois. Wracking my brain for a topic, I decided to write out the practical, sensible things I had learned about teaching, including things that weren't in those dry college textbooks on educational theory. To my amazement, my list of what successful teachers do was applauded at the end of my session. I kept playing with the idea of successful teaching, writing about strategies to survive and thrive in the classroom.

I have given my talk, *A Dozen Things Successful Teachers Do*, in many different venues. In 2015, I updated the talk yet again and delivered it to several groups of teachers in China. During one program, on a Saturday, in a very hot room, the teachers requested that I continue talking even after I had delivered the longest version of the presentation I had ever given. They wanted more? How could that be possible? Their questions were challenging me, making me reflect on how to help teachers feel successful, especially teachers faced with seemingly insurmountable issues in their schools.

So it was definitely time to sit down, do some research, and do more than just "play" with the idea of success in teaching. This book is the result of all those talks at professional development programs, my years of teaching, and the questions asked of me after my presentations.

What does success in teaching look like? There may be more questions than answers. Is success measured by perfect attendance of the teacher in a school year? Does teaching for thirty years make the teacher a success? Is it measured by students' test scores? Can the principal walk into a classroom and see success? Is it just a feeling? Do parents know which teachers are successful, and do they want their children in those teachers' rooms? Is being a successful teacher just a matter of keeping your sanity?

What will you, the reader, gain from this book? New teachers, both fully licensed and still in training, will get some survival skills. These skills include strategies, methods, and ideas to get your career started. As Parker Palmer has written, "Technique is what teachers use until the real teacher arrives" (1998, p. x). Having some techniques to rely on will help you get to 3:20 each day, and every Friday, feeling successful and sane.

Experienced teachers will get validation for what they have been doing. They will read sections of the book and say to themselves, "Aha! I've been doing that all along, but nobody ever complimented me on that." All teachers seek affirmation of their work, yet often little is given by administrators, colleagues, or communities. If you are considering dropping out of the teaching force, read this book to remember why you entered teaching in the first place.

Administrators need this book to better support their teachers. It is often said that the number one reason employees leave their jobs is that they don't feel supported by their bosses. In common language, people leave their jobs because they can't get along with their bosses. When principals, superintendents, and board members revisit the issues of teaching to better understand their teachers' work, a more positive work environment grows.

This book is designed to promote discussion and collegiality among teachers, administrators, and all who work in education. It can be read over a weekend and discussed by readers in a professional learning community (PLC) or by teachers over coffee. Contact me via e-mail (drmary clem@gmail.com) with your suggestions, and there may be a second dozen things that successful teachers do. We never know what's next in our careers in education!

Introduction

Teaching is a wonderful yet challenging profession. You probably remember your favorite teachers—the ones who engaged you in learning and knew you as a person. What did your favorite teachers do? What do effective teachers do? How do teachers become successful, and what are some things that successful teachers do? This book summarizes a dozen things that successful teachers do to ensure student success. It is a guide for new teachers as they start their careers as well as a set of good reminders for those who have been teaching a while.

Teaching is very hard work, and sometimes teachers ask themselves, "Why do I get up in the morning, go to work, and work so hard?" Successful teachers understand that it is necessary to have a personal philosophy for their work. What is your philosophy for doing the work of a teacher? How did you develop your philosophy? How do you motivate yourself to stay in your career until retirement?

Teachers realize that much preparation goes into learning how to be an effective teacher. Completion of a teacher-training program is, of course, the start to one's professional preparation. After completion of the program, a teacher should be a lifelong learner by reading journals, asking questions, observing other teachers, and listening to feedback when others observe them. When attending a workshop or program, it is important to learn at least one thing from each session. Teachers who attend professional development offerings and tell themselves that they will take away at least one thing do learn more.

When one gets a new class of students, it is too easy to see them all as a class and not as individuals. Many times, students arrive in a class, and they are not ready to learn or are behind academically. They may have social or emotional issues in their lives that limit their learning at a specific time. It is so important to get to know each student as an individual and see each student's strengths as well as weaknesses. We should observe our students and see what they can do, always looking for the positive.

In a classroom, there may be one or more students who try the patience of the teacher. One might even overhear a teacher say, "That student drives me crazy. I don't know whether to laugh or cry about him." Try to remember that the most challenging students are the ones who need their teachers the most. Be patient with these students, start each day fresh, and slowly win them over to trust you. As they trust you, and other adults more, their behavior and academic progress will improve.

How do you learn best? How do your students learn best? How can we teach so that all our students find a way to learn? Teaching with many different strategies addresses the issue of helping all students learn. As we teach, it is important to remember that students can learn by reading, memorizing, talking, presenting, watching, doing, practicing, singing, acting, writing, discussing, counting, and solving. So teachers can teach with strategies that engage students to learn in different ways.

Some teachers wonder about what exactly to tell parents in conferences or letters. Pretend that you are a parent. What would you want to know about your child's classroom, the lessons, and your child's achievement or behavior? If you would want to know, then other parents would want to know as well. Successful teachers know that outreach to families is very important.

Everyone needs help. In my work with teachers, I always say, "Teaching is too difficult a job to do alone. It is also too important a job to do alone." With this in mind, reach out to your colleagues for help and to give help and support. Sometimes, it is just a kind word that helps a colleague get through a tough day. Listening to another teacher helps even if we can't solve her problem.

When asked what my personal philosophy on teaching is, I often say, "I teach because I see the hope an education brings." Education is critically important in today's world, and what teachers do every day is VERY important work. Success in teaching is achievable in many ways. Our sense of efficacy—knowing that we can succeed and that we can reach students—starts the journey to success. The practical steps for success, as well as the mildly philosophical ones, are discussed in the chapters of this book.

WHEN READING THIS BOOK

Some readers will want to read the book from the beginning to the end, in order. It's just the way that some people think. Others can go to the chapter that they think best suits their need at this time. I might recommend that this book not be read alone but rather as a book study so that teachers can discuss it over a period of several weeks. Collegiality and a sense of camaraderie are missing in many schools, so using this book as a stimulus for building a cohesive faculty is an idea for its use.

Administrators at all levels in the school district need this book as a reminder of what teachers are doing in their work and what they are feeling about their work. I highly recommend the book for school board members, especially those who come to board work from the business world. Should parents of school-aged children read the book? Definitely, if they want insight into the world of the professionals who might spend more time with their children in the course of a week than they do. In short, this book is for those who teach, those who lead teachers' work, and those who want to know what today's teachers are experiencing.

Chapter One

Prepare Personally and Professionally

A successful teacher knows that there is no such thing as being overprepared.

In the 1940s my mother taught in a one-room school in central Illinois. She taught a dozen students, aged kindergarten to eighth grade. She kept the building and the outhouse clean, stoked the coal stove in the winter, and led the children in singing and exercise. What was her training? She had a high school diploma, a summer course in teaching, and an extraordinary work ethic. She simply taught as she had been taught in the one-room school she had attended. Was it enough preparation? I think my mother achieved success with her students, but in today's world, much more preparation is needed.

WHAT PREPARATION DO SUCCESSFUL TEACHERS HAVE?

Several years ago, a student said to me, "Why do I have to take all these education classes, like classes in reading. I know how to read, and I certainly read better than the second graders I plan to teach." She, like many people in the general public, had no idea that the teaching of reading involves a very different set of skills than just knowing how to read. Successful teachers prepare to teach because teaching is a very demanding job!

Successful teachers have training that matches their teaching assignments. They have the proper certifications and endorsements for their states. Teacher education provides both theoretical and practical training. Highly successful teachers know that they must continue their training after graduating from their education programs. Here is a quick review of teacher preparation.

It is important to note that every state in the United States has different rules for teacher certification. This is because the Constitution of the United States gives all rights to the states that are not specified in the Constitution. Yes, this is quite different than other countries, where teacher preparation is nationalized, coming to universities from their federal government. Because of this, teachers in the United States are first certified in the state where they complete teacher education/training. Then, they can apply for certification elsewhere.

Teacher Certification/Licensure

While there is no easy way to become a certificated, licensed teacher, the most straightforward path to earning teacher credentials is to major in an education program as an undergraduate student. In most states, teacher licensure can be earned during a four-year undergraduate program. (In this book, teacher licensure and certification are used interchangeably, as the language varies state to state.) If a student majors in a discipline and doesn't pursue teacher education concurrently, then a two-year program after graduation will lead to teacher certification.

What courses prepare candidates for their teaching credentials?

1. An introductory course that covers the foundations of education, how to earn teaching credentials, and a survey of the demographics of today's students.
2. Educational psychology—where future teachers learn about the cognitive, emotional, and social development of students as well as the science behind how students learn.
3. Diversity/multiculturalism—an in-depth course about the many races and cultures of the students in today's classrooms.
4. Courses in curriculum—learning what should be taught in the schools and how that material should be organized.
5. Courses in methods of teaching—how to teach the content material.
6. Classroom organization and management. This course covers how to organize a classroom, create procedures and routines, and implement rules and consequences.
7. Teaching students with special needs, also called teaching students with exceptionalities. This course introduces teachers to methods to meet the needs of all students, including those with learning and behavioral disabilities.
8. Field experience and student teaching/internship. To apply the theory learned in the classroom, teacher education candidates need real-life experience out in schools.

Some programs may include additional coursework in specialized reading courses, multicultural education, teaching students who are English language learners, or teaching gifted students. Adding coursework in applied behavioral analysis (ABA) is becoming another positive line on a teacher's résumé, as so many of today's students need interventions for their challenging behaviors.

Are there shortcuts to getting a classroom teaching job? Yes, there are alternative routes to certification as well as some short-term training that leads to temporary teaching positions. Teach for America (teachforamerica.org) recruits top college seniors and provides summer training before placing students in high-needs schools. Teachers in this program work for two years, and if they decide on teaching as a career, they must then enter a teacher certification program. Some states offer their own version of a similar program to get teachers into high-needs teaching fields quickly but generally for a short period of work until those teachers can earn full certification.

Do Successful Teachers Have a Master's Degree?

Once certificated (also commonly called certified), many teachers ask themselves, "Should I get a master's degree, and if so, how?" There are many routes to a master's degree. Teachers seeking the degree should search for a college or online program with the same process that they sought the institution for their bachelor's degrees. Good questions to ask when seeking a master's program include:

1. What is the total cost of tuition?
2. How long will this program take to complete? Are classes scheduled so that I can keep my teaching job and complete the degree in a timely manner?
3. How many of the classes are delivered as blended or online classes?
4. What is the reputation of the institution and the program itself?
5. Will I have an advisor, and how may I contact this person?
6. What do other teachers say about the work and instruction in this program?
7. Does my district/state recognize a degree from this program?
8. What area should my master's degree be in? Should I get a general degree in curriculum and instruction or one that is more specialized? For example, a master's in reading may add an additional certification to a teaching license, providing the teacher with new job opportunities.
9. Should I get my degree in leadership/administration to move into a higher-paying administrative job?
10. What will my salary be after completion of the degree?

The best advice is to talk with others in the school about how they earned their graduate degrees and to make sure that your degree leads to the new job or pay raise that you seek. While online degrees are more readily recognized than ever before, some are still not considered valid by all school districts. Online degrees may cost more than degrees that are on campus. Seek answers to your questions before starting a program.

Just over half of all public school teachers hold a master's degree, and approximately 38 percent of private school teachers do (www.facethefacts usa.org/facts/private-or-public-schools-whos-ahead-by-degrees). For practicing teachers seeking a different job within the education field or a pay raise for staying in the classroom, a graduate degree has become a requirement.

When should a teacher get a master's degree? The single best answer to this question is, "get the advanced degree when it is possible for you to do so." By choosing to stay one or two additional years in college, you can earn the degree before getting your first job. With a master's degree in hand, your starting salary will be higher, and you won't have to teach all day and go to college at night. Others choose to start teaching and then work on the degree. With some experience, the master's courses may be more relevant, or the teacher may have decided to study educational administration/leadership to change jobs within education.

PREPARATION TO GET, AND KEEP, A TEACHING JOB

Much has been written about teachers as lifelong learners, and being a continual learner is needed to thrive in education. After a master's degree, teachers continue to take classes and attend workshops and eventually share their knowledge by mentoring new teachers or teaching their colleagues. Becoming a leader in the school allows teachers to feel valued for their experience and work.

Maintaining membership in a professional organization can be of tremendous value for staying current in the field of education. Successful teachers are probably members of more than one organization. The discipline-specific organizations, such as the International Reading Association or the National Council of Teachers of Mathematics, provide updates on both content and pedagogy. Being a member of Kappa Delta Pi supports teachers with all areas of their professional work.

Reading the journals of the professional associations keeps teachers "in the know" about trends and issues. These associations have online resources, including blogs and social media sites, where teachers can communicate with others around the world. Need a lesson plan right this minute? Try the website of your professional association.

How Do I Get My First, and Next, Job in Education?

Long gone are the days when teachers got hired because they simply student-taught in a building. In times of teacher surplus and teacher shortage, candidates must present themselves professionally. Résumés must be tailored to each job advertisement, and candidates need to prepare extensively for behavior-based interviewing (BBI) style questions (Clement, 2013). Paperwork remains the key to getting noticed for a job. Even though paperwork is now electronic, candidates still need a résumé, cover letter, and portfolio.

The résumé is you at a glance, and a glance is all that is read initially by employers. The best key for getting your résumé to float to the top of a pile is to ensure that the top half of the first page of the résumé includes your certification and experience and something special about your career. For example:

> Professional Profile: During my six years of teaching fourth and fifth grades in a Title I school, I have raised test scores in all of my classes by at least 8 percent on the CCAT tests. Mentoring a student teacher and implementing a PLC with my colleagues have improved collegiality throughout our building.

This profile at the top of a résumé is certainly better than the traditional job objective statement: Seeking an elementary school position in fourth or fifth grade. Computer sorting software reads résumés for vocabulary that matches the job description, so candidates need to ensure that their résumés are tailored to each job advertisement. Employers seek past experiences that match their current needs, so teachers should include specific examples in their résumés of student successes and then elaborate on one or two of those successes in a cover letter. (See, for example, https://www.neamb.com/professional-resources/how-to-create-a-professional-profile-that-gets-you-noticed.htm.)

Teacher Job Interviews

Both first-time and experienced job seekers should prepare for behavior-based interviews. Behavior-based interviewing (BBI) is a style of interviewing that has come to education from the business world and is built on the premise that past behavior is the best predictor of future performance. To prepare for this type of interview, a teacher should practice explaining past successes with students in previous classrooms.

BBI questions start with the phrases "tell about a time when," "how have you," "describe how you have," or "what has been your approach to." When asked this style of question, a job candidate should have an example ready to share. The content of the questions includes all areas of teaching—classroom management, curriculum, methods, assessment, communication with families, meeting students' needs, and ability to work with colleagues. Sample BBI-style questions follow:

1. Explain how you have organized a classroom in the past, including a description of the procedures and routines you have developed for students.
2. Describe a classroom management plan that you have used that was successful. (What were the basic rules, consequences, and positive reinforcements?)
3. Tell about an individual lesson that you have taught that went well and why it went well.
4. How have you incorporated standards into your long-term curriculum planning?
5. Describe the student diversity in your most recent teaching experience and how you have met the needs of those students.
6. How have you communicated with parents/families about their students' work?
7. Describe your work with colleagues and your past supervisors.
8. What do you consider one of your best successes with students? Why?

Depending on the position, questions may be very subject- or grade-level specific. For example:

1. Our middle school classes are now using laptops in lieu of textbooks. Describe your experience with technology in the classroom.
2. How have you prepared third-grade students for the state's standardized tests in reading and math?
3. What are some tried-and-true methods for getting eleventh grade students to pass the required US history course?
4. In this position, approximately 25 percent of the class will be English language learners (ELLs). What is your experience teaching ELLs?

The best advice for preparing for a teacher job interview is to know as much about the school and district as possible. Never ask a question of the interviewer that is information found on their website. It is, however, a good idea to reference their website at some point in the interview. For example, "I read on your website that each of the schools' principals recommends a book for students and parents to read together each month. I haven't seen this done before and look forward to being a part of this principal/teacher/parent reading program."

How else should candidates prepare for a job interview? All teachers should practice answers to possible questions by speaking aloud in front of a mirror. Candidates may want to practice their answers while speaking to a person so that they may also practice eye contact and nonverbal responses.

There are two mnemonics that guide candidates in their answers—PAR and STAR. PAR represents problem, action, and result. This helps candidates when a question is asked about a problem. If the candidate is asked "Tell us about a time when a student disrupted your teaching and what you did about it," he or she can phrase an answer with PAR. The sample answer might be as follows:

> In my seventh-grade language arts classroom, blurting out is a recurring problem because students this age want to be heard and want attention. I often use think-pair-share to guide students' responses so they don't disrupt by shouting out answers. Before I even ask a question, I tell students that they will have silent time to think of their answer and then they can pair with a partner to discuss their answers. Finally, we will share the very best answers. This works well.

What do employers really want to know about candidates? They want to know that you can do the many jobs required of teachers. They want to hear you talk about your past successes with students. They want to know that you can organize a classroom and establish good classroom management. Principals want to hire energetic new people who will revitalize their faculty. After all, they probably have enough burned-out teachers!

Principals want teachers who can not only get along with their colleagues but also lead their colleagues. Starting a professional learning community (PLC) and helping other teachers learn how to study issues together are great assets for a new hire. The school administrator wants to hire people who will volunteer when needed for both small and larger duties. Teachers who can train a student teacher or mentor a new teacher are always needed.

Principals appreciate positive employees with a sense of humor! Teaching is a challenging job, and there are many tough, stressful days. While an employer should understand that it's OK to complain a bit, no one wants to work with the chronic complainer. Handling the stress of teaching is part of the personal preparation that teachers need to develop.

Successful teachers find jobs that are a match with their training, expertise, beliefs, and philosophy. An interview is a two-way street. Teachers strive to sell their strengths but should also be listening to the interviewers to see whether the job is the best match for them. It is important to find, and have, supportive administrators to be successful. An interview is a time for the candidate to evaluate the level of support provided teachers in the potential new job.

Surprise Interview Questions

A private school principal uses this question to sort the commitment of new hires to the school: "If our school were to run out of money before the end of the school year, would you still teach here?" How would you answer? This principal believes that commitment is a big part of teacher success!

Some employers continue to ask candidates about their biggest weakness. This question is tough to answer. A strong candidate answers in a way that doesn't really point out a weakness but rather alludes to the candidate's ability to be humble and to continue growing as a professional. Examples follow:

1. I am not an expert at everything that a veteran teacher needs to know, but I do know that I need to continue learning. Just this year, I attended my first national conference for teachers, and my eyes were opened to the value of attending conferences. I learned that it was a weakness of mine that I hadn't joined a professional association or budgeted money to attend a conference before this year.
2. Sometimes, I take students' and parents' comments too personally. I need to listen to feedback and sort and edit it! I am a professional, and my hundreds of hours of field experience and student teaching do make me qualified to do the job of teaching.
3. Sometimes, I know an example for a question posed in a faculty meeting or have something pertinent to add, but I am hesitant to speak up. I do believe that listening is important, and I want to improve on how I speak up to share my expertise and experience.

Then, of course, are the employers who ask completely odd questions that are unrelated to teaching. They ask them to see whether they can throw you off guard, silence you, or see how resilient you are. These questions are generally worded as follows:

1. If you were a bird, which bird would you be, and why?
2. If you were an ice cream flavor, which would you be, and why?
3. If you were a plant, which one would you be, and why?
4. If you were a part of a car, which would you be, and why?

The best advice to answer any of these questions is to smile, laugh lightly, and make up an answer. One candidate answered the car part question with this line: "I would be the steering wheel because I am a leader, steering my students in the right direction." Another candidate said, "I would be the eagle soaring with my students. And, by the way, I know a great website where students can watch an eagle's nest when we do our unit on birds." Be creative and continue to be confident when you answer crazy questions.

Getting Your Next Job

A colleague of mine once quipped that your first day on a new job is also the first day that you start preparing for your next job. While you might consider this a pessimistic view, there are things that every teacher should consider about his or her future jobs.

Keeping good records is a way to be ready for a job move. Make portfolios every year of your success stories. In fact, keep some tables of how many students you teach each year, the preparations you have had for multiple classes, and test score results. It is much more impressive to tell a future employer that you have worked with 6,324 students over an eight-year period than to just say that you have taught eight years.

Keep files with student and parent comments. In a cover letter to a future employer, you can add one or two lines from these comments. It personalizes your application materials and greatly enhances your chances of having your paperwork noticed for an interview. Keep student work samples and build a portfolio to take to your next job interview. (Remember to remove all names and data that could be traced to individual students.)

Build a network of people who can write letters of recommendations for you. While recommendations are done electronically now, employers still need to see what your past bosses and colleagues have to say about you. In addition to your principal, consider getting recommendations from a colleague who worked with you on a committee, someone that you mentored, and perhaps even a trusted parent.

The Personal Preparation Needed for Teaching

Motivational speaker Matt Jones wrote that "The number one thing you can do to improve yourself professionally is to improve yourself personally" (2016, p. 38). Teachers who "get their ducks in a row" in their personal lives tend to have better school years, too.

Often advertised as the "family-friendly" profession, teaching does offer employees the opportunity to work the same hours and weeks as their school-aged children. This is very different than some jobs in the business world. Working for a corporation, it would not be uncommon for an employee to get a call on Saturday, informing her or him to leave on Sunday and fly across the country to a job site and to stay there until the job was finished or the problem resolved. Teachers go to the same work site each week, and the travel demands are almost nonexistent.

Teachers are needed everywhere—small towns, big cities, and suburban areas. When a spouse relocates for a job, a teacher has much more flexibility than some professionals with regard to finding a new job. In our household, my husband, a broadcast systems engineer, must work where network television originates—New York City, large cities in California, or Atlanta. Fortunately, I can teach in any of these three areas.

In my work with adult job changers who seek to enter teaching from other professions, a large percentage are women striving to find jobs that balance work and home life. Many are recently divorced women who need a way to support a family and still have time to be with their children. Some research has found that just over three-fourths of the teaching force in the United States is female (https://nces.ed.gov/fastfacts/display.asp?id=28).

If teaching is family friendly, why do teachers leave their positions? "About 51 percent of public school teachers who left teaching in 2012–2013 reported that the manageability of their work load was better in their current position than in teaching. Additionally, 53 percent of public school leavers reported that their general work conditions were better in their current position than in teaching" (https://nces.ed.gov/fastfacts/display.asp?id=28).

Teaching is, apparently, NOT for everyone. The general public often perceives the teacher's workday to be 8 to 3 because that is when the students are in attendance. What the public doesn't see is the hours and hours of time spent on planning, grading, and organizing after the students leave. Teachers do spend a lot of time on the weekends preparing for the next week. As one teacher quipped, "It's the worrying that takes the most time. I constantly worry about how to get all the children to succeed, to do better, and to behave. I worry about the testing, my own evaluations, and how I am going to have the energy to keep doing this job I love."

Loewus (2017) wrote that the average US teacher worked 53 hours a week in 2017. One administrator said that education was a job that took 50 or 60 hours a week to do well but at least there was some flexibility in the 50 or 60 hours the teachers chose to work. In other words, teachers could decide to come to work early, stay late, take work home, or do work over the weekend. Hopefully, they wouldn't choose to do all of those!

Stress Management and Personal Preparation

Stress is inevitable in any job, and stress in teaching may be at an all-time high. Mazzone and Miglionico (2014) reported that "Only two percent of teachers reported that they are not experiencing stress on the job" (p. 2). Teachers are concerned about their evaluations and re-employment. They worry about curricular changes and imposed teaching methods or programs as well as standardized testing and student achievement. Stressed teachers may not be as successful because of absenteeism, lower morale, and attitude (Clement, 2017a; Clement, 2017b).

Just how do teachers manage their stress and prepare personally for their teaching? Successful teachers recognize that they have to care for their own well-being. A healthy lifestyle, including proper diet, exercise, and sleep, really is essential. Eat from the salad bar, go for a walk, and take a sick day when you are sick!

The three key steps for stress management sound so simple.

1. Identify the stressors in your job and personal life.
2. Write out what you could do to lower those stressors.
3. Do what you just wrote out! Implement the action needed.

However, doing these three steps is hard. For example, a teacher complained that a huge stress in her life was always hosting Thanksgiving dinner. A professional stress counselor suggested that she not host the meal but rather tell the extended family members that this year's celebration would be a potluck at someone else's home or even in a rented community space. The teacher looked horrified and replied, "Oh no, I could never do that." "Well," commented the counselor, "then you will always have that stress." Do you see the point? While teachers can't change the curriculum or the stressors imposed at school, they can change some things within their personal lives.

No One Can Do It All

After the birth of her child, a good friend of mine asked me how I thought other women balanced marriage, motherhood, and careers. I replied that many don't do so successfully or optimally. Many parents, both mothers and fathers, get everything done but are truly too busy and too stressed for many years of their lives. Successful professionals need to prioritize. For some, that means stopping out of their job for a few years, working part-time, or enlisting the help of their own parents for childcare.

Many teachers with children are super organized and make to-do lists for all family members. Yes, children can run a washing machine (after a certain age) and can help with dishes and picking up the house. It takes planning to have a well-run home, just as it takes planning for a well-run classroom.

It is indeed a myth that people can do everything at every stage of their life. Recognizing that there are only so many hours in a day is important! Of course, when I have taught stress management, many teachers have contested my recommendations saying that they must earn a living to pay their bills. I agree, as I must do so, also. I do not, however, have to host every holiday meal for the extended family every year. Sometimes saying no yields more opportunities to say yes and remain balanced. What is the bottom line? Successful teachers have found the balance that works for them with regard to their personal lives. It is different for everyone.

The last chapters of this book will also provide insights and ideas for getting support for teachers' work through collegial relationships, networks, and personal strength.

KEYS FOR SUCCESS

1. Successful teachers have proper training and certifications that match their jobs.
2. Successful teachers, when interviewing for teaching jobs, need to explain past successes but also seek to know whether the job is right for them.
3. Successful teachers know that earning a master's degree can lead to higher pay and better preparation.
4. Successful teachers know that continued learning is necessary in teaching.
5. Successful teachers know that preparing personally is as important as preparing professionally.
6. Successful teachers find balance in their lives and know when to say no so that they are not overwhelmed. No one can do everything.
7. Successful teachers plan for their future jobs. They build networks of employers and colleagues to help them get their next job.

Chapter Two

Know Educational Psychology

Successful teachers know about their students—their development, how they learn, and what motivates them.

When one gets a new class of students, it is too easy to see them all as a class and not as individuals. Many times, students arrive in a class, and they are not ready to learn or are behind academically. They may have social or emotional issues in their lives that limit their learning at a particular time. It is so important to get to know each student as an individual and see each student's strengths as well as weaknesses. We should observe our students and see what they can do, always looking for the positive.

In addition to teaching subject material, the teacher works to teach students how to be students. We should not assume that students know the basic procedures and routines of school until we teach them in each classroom. Good classrooms have a feel as a family might, with students getting along well with each other and helping each other. The teacher sets the tone for the classroom and teaches the students how to get along well with each other.

In a classroom, there may be one or more students who try the patience of the teacher. One might even overhear a teacher say, "Student X drives me crazy. I don't know whether to laugh or cry about him." I try to remember that the most challenging students are the ones who need their teachers the most. Be patient with these students, start each day fresh, and slowly win them over to trust you. As they trust you, and other adults, more, their behavior and academic progress will improve. Learning to accept all students may come naturally to some, but for the rest of us, a sound grounding in educational psychology will guide us to success.

Chapter 2

WHY EDUCATIONAL PSYCHOLOGY?

When I first started teaching educational psychology, students asked why they needed that class, especially since Psych 101 was already a college requirement. Now, I start each semester explaining why the course will help them to be successful teachers.

Educational psychology is all about development—the cognitive, personal, social, and emotional development of students. It's the course where future teachers learn about learning and motivation. Teachers need to know about IQ and EQ (emotional intelligence), about operant and classical conditioning, and about reinforcement of learning and applied behavioral analysis. Successful teachers don't teach below or above students' levels. They know how short- and long-term memory work and how to help their students construct knowledge.

Even when a future teacher forgets just exactly what Bandura or Piaget or Vygotsky contributed to the knowledge base of teaching, that's OK. If teachers remember that not all students learn the same way at the same time, that building trusting relationships with students is critically important, and that deep learning takes time, they are on the road to success.

DEVELOPMENT

I often hear parents say that their child is "five going on fifteen" or that their middle school child could pass for a college freshman. My twenty-year-old college students complete field experiences in area schools, come back to campus, and report that "today's kids are not like we were." Really? They are twenty and say that sixteen-year-olds are vastly different than they were.

One of my favorite workshop activities is to ask teachers what their students are like. I ask them to write out three adjectives or short, descriptive phrases about their students. Here is a sample of what I have heard:

- Talkative, noisy, incapable of sitting still or being quiet
- Wise beyond their years
- Living in poverty and it shows
- Restless
- Social, very social
- Raised by TV and the Internet
- Anxious, many clinically so
- Street smart
- Mature looking, but immature acting
- Lacking basic reading and writing skills
- Big dreamers

- Wanting it all

When we look at this list, many items jump out as ones that savvy teachers can help students with, especially with knowledge of developmental levels of students. For example, a kindergarten teacher shouldn't expect a five-year-old to be able to sit still very long, so she must incorporate movement into lessons. She may have students stand and sing numbers, and they may jump at every multiple of five.

Middle school students are very social, wanting to talk all the time. So let them! The key is to have them talking about their work and assignments in short, monitored bursts of time. High school students may lead the lives of young adults—with jobs, cars, and maybe even children of their own. For these students, the teacher has to make the relevance of each lesson clear. Let's look at more specifics of student development.

Physical and Brain Development

A former colleague of mine visited his pregnant daughter often and gave her books to read to her child before the child's birth. This professor of literacy proudly displayed a picture of himself reading to his grandchild when the child was less than a week old. That was an educationally stimulating environment for a child.

The brain develops well in a stimulating environment early in life. What about students who experience extreme deprivation early in life instead of a supportive, stimulating environment? Those students may have negative effects from their first years of life that we, as teachers, continue to see in the grade we teach. So what do we do?

Teachers can offer the most supportive environment possible. Enrichment activities and continuous reading lessons help students to increase learning. The brain's capacity for growth is tremendous, so exposing students to more learning experiences is critically important for growth. Instead of cutting back on the curriculum, increasing it and including reading skills in all classes can be an answer to remediate deficiencies in children's early years.

When teachers know that the brain has plasticity—and can be shaped by reading, activities, and experiences—they can plan lessons accordingly. However, it might be prudent to read deeply about so-called brain-based learning before jumping on the bandwagon to teach to students' right and left brains. There remains much debate about the research on brain-based learning. As one of my college professors said years ago, "Use your left brain or your right brain to learn this. I don't care which side of your brain you use, but use your brain. I mean, really, which other bodily organ will you use to learn? Not your gall bladder." (But I do encourage teachers to read the brain-based research and decide what to take from it and use.)

Teachers of adolescents and teenagers need to know that psychology can keep them a step ahead of their students. This group of students is in a developmental stage where taking risks and seeking thrills are a natural part of life. Don't fight students in this stage of development, but rather capitalize on it with assignments that may tap into their passion and energy.

Research in educational psychology tells us that teenagers need nine hours of sleep a night (Woolfolk, 2016, pp. 38–39). Now, really, how many of them go to bed early enough to get that much sleep? What does this mean for teachers? It means that those teaching first-period classes need to have very active classes, or even some of the most well-intentioned high school students will fall asleep. Active learning will be important for students in this developmental stage.

Cognitive and Social Development

Every teacher has probably studied the theories of Jean Piaget and can recite his cognitive development stages: sensorimotor, preoperational, concrete operational, and formal operational. However, any veteran teacher will tell you that just because a student's age places him or her in a certain stage, that doesn't necessarily mean that the student will think and problem solve as that stage of development suggests.

Knowing the developmental stages of our students, with Piaget's stages or the research of others, can help teachers not to teach above or below students' developmental level. Elementary students are concrete thinkers and generally like hands-on problems. Older adolescents should be able to think scientifically and solve abstract problems. However, students at all developmental stages need guidance with problem solving and learning to think logically.

A colleague of mine recently said that "18 is the new 15." He felt that eighteen-year-olds were not as mature as they used to be and that their learning seemed to be well behind his expectations for high school seniors. Have societal norms changed the developmental levels of students? It's a good question that merits more research.

On the other hand, I also know the parents of a fifteen-year-old who report that their daughter could pass for a college student, not the high school freshman that she is. Her physical development is well above the standard expected, but her academic level and handwriting might make a teacher think she was a fifth-grader. What does this say about the development of students? How does a teacher help and support this student in the classroom? Does this student need some counseling intervention to deal with the discrepancy of her physical development versus her cognitive development? (Answer: I think so!) The bottom line is to know that all students develop at different levels and we need to take that in to consideration to meet their needs.

LEARNING

Those who study to be teachers take a course or courses in educational psychology to know how students learn. When we know the basics of how learning works, we can teach better.

Ask yourself these questions about your own learning:

1. How do you learn best?
2. Do you prefer to study alone or with others?
3. Which subjects or topics were particularly easy for you to learn as a student?
4. Which subjects or topics were particularly hard for you to learn as a student?
5. Now, as a teacher, why do you think those subjects and topics were easy or hard?
6. Was reading easy or hard for you as a student? Is reading easy or hard for you today?
7. Is memorizing easy or hard for you?
8. Do you like to learn by hearing a teacher go step by step through directions?
9. Do you prefer to learn by figuring things out on your own?
10. Do you like to see visuals when someone is talking/teaching/presenting important new material?
11. How is your test anxiety? What made you feel prepared for tests as a student?
12. What makes you frustrated as a learner today? What made you frustrated as a learner when you were a student?
13. Did you feel bored in your classes as a student?
14. Did you feel overwhelmed in your classes as a student?
15. If you were to rank yourself against your classmates at different stages of your education, how would you rank yourself? Does it matter how you compared to your classmates? Should it?

Now, as a teacher, which of the questions from this list would you want to ask your students? Remembering students' developmental levels, an interest inventory about a student's learning will look very different for elementary, middle, and high school students. Some examples follow.

For elementary students:

1. What do you like to do in class?
2. What was a favorite activity in last year's class?
3. What activities aren't your favorites?
4. Do you like to read?
5. How much do you read outside of class?
6. What is easy or fun for you to learn?
7. What is a challenge or hard for you to learn?
8. What would you like the teacher to do more of in the class?
9. What would you like the teacher to do less of in the class?
10. What would you like to tell the teacher about school?

For middle school students:
For each of the following, rate your response on a scale of 1 to 5, where 1 is no interest and 5 is high interest. If you want to do more of something in class, give that topic a 5.

1. Challenging work in the classroom
2. Group work
3. Working on a computer
4. Reading
5. Working on my own

Now, please provide a short answer:

1. Which activities and lessons from last year interested you the most?
2. Which activities and lessons from last year interested you the least?
3. How do you learn best (in math, in social studies, in science)?
4. What is your strongest subject, and why do you think you are strongest in that subject?
5. What would you like the teacher to know about how you like to learn?

For secondary students:
For each of the following, rate your response on a scale of 1 to 5, where 1 is no interest and 5 is high interest. If you want to do more of the topic listed, give it a 5.

1. Working on teams or in groups
2. Working independently
3. Spending time on a computer
4. Reading
5. Doing challenging work to prepare me for college

Now, please provide a short answer:

1. How do you learn best?
2. What can the teacher do to help you learn this subject material?
3. How much do you study outside of class?
4. How strong do you think your reading skills are?
5. How strong do you think your study skills are?
6. Do you feel you will be ready for college-level work?

Vygotsky and the ZPD

Every educational psychology class has a lesson or two about Lev Vygotsky (1896–1934) and his work. He studied learning and the development of students to improve his own teaching. His theories include how students construct learning and meaning. His work is considered to be a sociocultural perspective, and he is most famous for the theory of the Zone of Proximal Development (ZPD). ZPD is "the area between the child's current performance (the problems the child can solve independently without any support) and the level of performance that the child could achieve with adult guidance" (Woolfolk, 2016, p. 61). In other words, the ZPD is where students can learn best. It's the wonderful spot between what students can do on their own and what they can do with help/teaching.

The next questions should be, "How do we know what students can do?" and "How do we know just how much to present, teach, and have students do before they are too overwhelmed to learn?" And what if the mandated curriculum is way out of the student's zone, or even the average zone of the whole class?

The strategy of scaffolding is used to teach students so that they build knowledge based on what they already know. It involves assisting the learner and guiding participation. Teachers can scaffold with prompts, reminders, and giving just enough information in chunks so that the students are following the content of the lesson. Giving feedback to students as they work helps students to know whether they are on the right track. Listening to student feedback and their questions allows the teacher to understand exactly where the students are in mastering material.

Some have called the Zone of Proximal Development the "magic middle." It's where students are challenged, but not overwhelmed. Here's an example that most people can relate to if they have ever studied a foreign language:

> The Spanish teacher walks in to the classroom of a beginning, first-year Spanish class and speaks only in Spanish. She never uses English, not even to explain the classroom rules or homework. Students are overwhelmed and even

college students have been known to cry in this situation. This is a clear-cut example of not being in the students' ZPD.

However, if a Spanish teacher speaks the language 85 to 90 percent of the time and uses the students' previous knowledge of how English works to reinforce concepts and grammar, this indicates scaffolding. It also lowers the students' fear of language learning enough for them to actually start learning.

Foreign language is not the only subject that students fear or hate instantly. Think about your own experiences. Which subject was the one that gave you fear? For many it is math, and for others it is chemistry. It might be argued that the shortage of physics teachers and physicists is because of the fact that students stay as far away from physics classes as they possibly can. Many high school and college students avoid any class where they fear they might not earn an A or a B. If a class, any class, can be taught in the students' ZPD and in a way that lowers the fear and anxiety of the students, then learning can take place.

Some issues of learning are because of lack of developmental readiness or lack of previous experience. A preschool student was evaluated as being in need of special help because of things he couldn't do. One of the tests was cutting with scissors. When the evaluator spoke to the mother, she replied, "Of course, he can't cut with scissors. I haven't let him touch them because of his age."

Teachers can help students learn by building their background knowledge with basics. Add visuals to lessons and teach a lot of vocabulary. Provide video clips to show students what they might never have seen before coming in to your class. Present new material without shaming students for not knowing it already. After they have had direct instruction, provide problems and activities for group work where students can support each other's learning.

Intelligence and Teaching Students

Intelligence is a basic ability. It affects performance on cognitive (thinking) tasks. Intelligence involves our ability to transfer knowledge and to apply what we know to something new. Howard Gardner's work on multiple intelligences has been considered seminal in the field for helping teachers get students to learn by addressing multiple intelligences in their lessons. Many teachers have taken the idea of multiple intelligences and used it to improve instruction in their classrooms. There is also backlash on the theory of multiple intelligences. Teachers need to know about this theory or any other theory or body of research to see whether they can take an idea and apply it to their teaching.

With regard to the work of Howard Gardner, he has suggested eight or nine intelligences (See, for a summary, Woolfolk, 2016, or do an online search for more information.). Recognizing multiple intelligences can be a real "aha" moment for teachers and a great help to them as they accept all learners and teach them. As a teacher, have you seen students who were naturally stronger in music, or logic, or language? Are some students just automatically good at interpersonal communication?

When I read about multiple intelligences, I immediately start diagnosing myself. I think my linguistic, interpersonal, and intrapersonal skills are strong and may be what helped me to initially succeed in school. Much of early school success has been traditionally attributed to reading, writing, and linguistic skills. I could also "read" what my teachers wanted—an interpersonal skill. I know I can't juggle, which is a bodily kinesthetic skill, and I was never a good dancer. What if I had taken dance classes as a three-year-old? Would an early intervention have improved my "intelligence" in this area?

The psychology of intelligence and multiple intelligences is important to know. It helps teachers to understand their students, respect their strengths, and work on the weaker areas. The big point that successful teachers know is that they have to help all students improve in all areas. A brilliant student in math will also need some interpersonal skills to become an engineer. A student who exhibits strong naturalist skills, loving plants and the outdoors, will still need math skills to run a greenhouse and earn a living.

I once heard a graduate student say that her eyes glazed over any time anyone said the word "cognitive." I tell my students to substitute the word *thinking* when they read *cognitive* and see if that makes sense. Cognitive is an adjective that describes nouns referring to the process of knowing or perceiving. Teachers need to know the students' cognitive development so that we can meet them in the right spot—the magic middle, or the ZPD. Successful teachers recognize that their students are intelligent, with many strengths of varying intelligences, and that teaching in a variety of ways helps individual students learn.

Memory

Even before I went to kindergarten, one of my aunts thought I could read. My mother had read one of my favorite storybooks to me over and over, and I had virtually memorized the lines on the page after hearing the story so often. I pulled out the little book to "read" it to my aunt and missed very few words. My memory at age four was pretty good! I could also memorize nursery rhymes, people's names, where I kept things in my room, and TV jingles. I could sing the theme song from the old TV show *The Beverly Hillbillies* completely through after hearing it a few times.

A few years ago, after a long plane flight, I was in line to get a rental car. When the attendant asked for my phone number, I drew a blank and had to get out my phone and look it up. How was it possible that I didn't remember my own phone number when I could always remember everything? How does memory work, and what should teachers know about memory and learning?

Memory is tremendously important for learning. As a foreign language teacher, I did memory drills every day so that my students could learn Spanish. I had a few students who said, "I really want to be fluent in Spanish and to speak it well, but I do not want to memorize verb endings or vocabulary words." I used to think that a comment like this just meant that the student didn't want to put in the effort to learn. However, memory's role in learning is more complicated than that.

We have a working memory and a long-term memory. Our working memory lets us remember the gate we are to walk to at the airport. After the flight leaves, we don't need to know the gate, so it is not in long-term memory. Our long-term memory allows us to remember what we can and can't carry in our carry-on bags on the plane. If we fly a lot, knowing that matters.

Let me continue the travel analogy a bit. There is also episodic memory. This is a memory tied to a time and place. I like episodic memory because I travel a lot. I have been to the top of the Eiffel Tower multiple times, with different groups of people. When I finally got to Paris with my husband, we went to the top of the tower, and I started telling him about the people I was with on my tour several years ago. I didn't remember their names until I stood where I had stood with them. The episode came back to me when I was there. My husband was also amazed that I knew which bus and metro lines would take us to within a block of our hotel. I had done this route in Paris twice before and "remembered" when I got there.

So how does knowing about memory help us to teach students better? Application of learning requires that we learn some things to automaticity. This means that we know it "cold" and can apply what we know. When students memorize verb endings in Spanish, they can then make sentences and start conversations. When they know automatically that "yo" is I, then they can say "Yo tengo mi libro" (I have my book). Now, for the magic bullet that makes memorization work. The student has to have a *reason* to know how to say "I have a book." In a foreign language class, savvy teachers make the learning very real by having students talk about themselves, having real conversations, and doing things in the language from the start of the course. The opposite of this is when I first learned French. We had to memorize dialogues from the book. I often said the lines in French: "Hello, I am John Cluny. I love to ski in the Alps." As a girl in the midwestern United States, was I ever going to need to say those lines?

Memory is what helps us know basic math facts "cold," and then we can progress to higher math. Knowing certain words "by sight" allows us to read well. This is why memory is important. When students are never taught how to memorize or never memorize nursery rhymes as a child, memorization may be hard for them. The teacher will need to teach how to memorize for a given subject. Mnemonics helps students to memorize. (Didn't we all learn the names of the Great Lakes of America by remembering HOMES?) Visuals help students to memorize. Practice and drills can be very useful—but don't overdo them.

Provide some episodic memory events to help students learn. I know from experience that when former students see me out in the community, they instantly say, "Hola, señora Clemente." After years and years, how do they remember my name? Every day, they used my Spanish name in class, and even if they have never spoken Spanish in over twenty-five years, they will still speak to me in Spanish. Yes, memorization to the level of automatic recall works!

There has been a backlash to memorization in the past twenty years, or perhaps longer. Many teachers no longer have students memorize multiplication tables because a calculator is as close as a cell phone. Very few students are ever asked to memorize stanzas of a poem. Alas, rarely do some young students ever hear a nursery rhyme, much less get to memorize one. While it may not be necessary to memorize the state capitals in alphabetical order, some memorization should be part of all classroom experiences because memory is critical to learning.

Now, why couldn't I remember my own phone number after the long flight? Have you ever *been* on a 14-hour flight? Many factors can interfere with memory and therefore learning. Being overly tired is one such interference. Being hungry, afraid, stressed, or overly worried about something else interferes with memory. Just being mad and upset can stop the learning. I was once required to attend an all-day workshop on my campus on a Friday when I had scheduled final student teaching observations out in the schools. My schedule was set weeks in advance, and being told I had to change my plans infuriated me. How much did I get out of the workshop? Not much. Now, remember that your students are required to be in your class—day in and day out, no matter their emotional state. It's no wonder achievement scores are not at the top of the charts.

When parents and teachers of very young children have them memorize little things, that experience helps students when they are older. When teachers make meaningful connections, organize information, provide images and situations (episodes), memorization is enhanced. Memorization is valuable in learning the basics and for building toward deeper learning.

Chapter 2
MOTIVATION

"John seems bright but is just not motivated to do his work." "Sarah is nice in class but appears to be unmotivated." "Terry can do good work but is unmotivated to do his work in the time frames needed." I'm afraid that millions of teachers have thought, said, or written lines similar to these about students.

I remember a student who I would have labeled as completely unmotivated in my high school class. One night, I saw her working at the concession stand during a football game, and she was not only rushing around but was a leader of others. I asked the concession stand sponsor about her work. "She's great," he said. "My most motivated student." What? I couldn't believe that her name and the word *motivated* could be used in the same sentence.

Successful teachers have learned that what motivates some students may totally bore others. Doing a song and dance to motivate students (literally or figuratively) may still not make some students interested in our subjects. Giving out candy may provide some extrinsic motivation, but it is not the way to truly motivate students. We want students to be excited about what we teach and to want to be at school and in our classrooms. Building that intrinsic motivation is a critical component to long-term learning.

I always introduce motivation to my teacher education students by asking them what motivates them to come to class twice a week. Is it the sheer pleasure of learning educational psychology? Is it their dedication to earning a teaching certificate, knowing that this is a required course? Is it self-discipline that gets them to class, or do they feel that if they skip class they are wasting their and their parents' tuition money?

As an aside, my former doctor once said to me that he never missed a single day of class during medical school because he was afraid he might miss something that would someday help him save a patient's life. That is fantastic intrinsic motivation, and I had complete trust in that doctor.

Today's teachers make use of a lot of extrinsic behavioral motivators. They include reinforcements, rewards, incentives, and also punishments. Students who are in a classroom with these types of motivators work to earn a reward or avoid the punishment. Teachers who strive for intrinsically motivated students tend to appeal to students' own goals and teach that one should enjoy the work, using it for self-actualization. After all, the need to feel competent, successful, and independent is important for all students, no matter their age.

What are some practical steps for motivating students that do not include candy, popcorn, ice cream, or trips to the "treasure chest"? Providing a rationale for what is done is often a first step for motivating students. Successful teachers say, "We are doing this today because . . . ," and they complete that sentence with something relevant. They do not say, "We are doing this today because you need to know it on the standardized test in March."

Communicating honestly with students helps to motivate them. Some kindergarten classes are now called "The graduating class of _____." Of course, the blank is filled in with a year that is twelve years in the future. Perhaps it might be more useful to have that communication be about something a bit closer, but I am all in favor of talking about high school graduation as early as possible.

Having goals is a motivator. Students can learn to set short-term goals and then discuss the value of having met the goal. Then, they can discuss long-term goals and dreams for the future. Bringing in speakers as role models can help students to set goals and see what they have to do to meet a goal. It's easy to say, "I'll be an engineer" or "I'll be a doctor," but students have to realize that to meet such a lofty goal, they must get a very good education—every year and every day.

What Can Detract from Motivation?

Every teacher whom I have ever known has seen at least one student who is work avoidant. This student does not try because he or she feels that there is no way to succeed at the task, much less excel at it. So rather than look stupid for not being able to meet expectations, the student simply does not attempt work or refuses to finish it. High school students have had years of failures in school to remind them that they won't be the best or the brightest. Even early elementary students avoid work, seemingly unmotivated, because they have already experienced failure or at least a lack of success.

Remember my experience with the totally unmotivated student who excelled at concession stand management? Little did I know that she aspired to run a restaurant and the teacher in charge of the concession stand had discovered this about her. He invited her to learn how to manage the stand, with the long-term goal of restaurant management. He praised her work, and she finally found success at something. Now, how do all teachers do this for students?

Part of success comes from learning the difference between talent and hard work. Even naturally talented people have to work hard to succeed. Students need to learn that rushing through work because someone told them they were smart is not the way to continue learning. Successful teachers praise effort, perseverance, and the energy expended by a student on tasks. They explain that deep learning takes time and work.

Is fear in the classroom a motivator? Yes, but let's not overdo it. I was in a graduate class where our professor said that the majority of prison inmates were either illiterate or poor readers and writers. So the professor proclaimed, "Should we tell students that if they don't learn to read well that they will end up in prison?" The answer is no, but it is an interesting story.

Here is another very personal example. When I was a little girl, my grandparents often took me to see my grandmother's sister and her family. This family lived in a very small, rural town in southern Illinois. On the road to my great-aunt's home, we passed by the home of a very poor family. They lived in a house that was literally beside a deep ditch, and their many children were often seen playing in the ditch and on the side of the highway. Every time we saw these children, my grandfather admonished, "This is what happens to children who don't study in school and listen to their teachers. They grow up to be poor and live in shacks by the side of the road. You don't want that to happen to you. Work hard in school."

My grandfather was often known to additionally admonish us about the value of school and its effect on our careers. He would say, "I have had to work hard all of my life on the farm. If you don't want to do back-breaking work all of your life, for little money, get a good education." Did his stories motivate me? Yes, they certainly did because I went to college for a total of eight years to earn three degrees. Is the fear approach the best motivator? Maybe not, but teachers can tell success stories and serve as role models for their students.

When teachers tap in to students' interests and curiosity, motivation may follow naturally. When a student likes dinosaurs, the elementary teacher may find books about dinosaurs to motivate the student to read. Letting students choose their books or how they complete an assignment can be motivational.

Teachers often ask, "But what do we do when the student is not interested in anything?" It's a valid question. Are teachers responsible for building the interest factors for their subjects? I heard Dave Burgess (2012), the author of *Teach Like a Pirate*, speak, and he does indeed find hooks for teaching his material in every class. He dresses the part of historical figures for his history classes. He builds sets in his room as a backdrop for the era in the chapters of the history book. He builds suspense into his lessons, like pulling a bright red bra out of a sack to teach about the women's movement of the 1960s. Can we all teach like that every day? Probably not, but we can all plan great lessons and consider what is in the lesson to motivate the students.

KEYS FOR SUCCESS

1. Successful teachers use psychology to better understand their students.
2. Successful teachers recognize developmental readiness and use scaffolding to support students who aren't quite ready to learn/do things on their own.
3. Successful teachers know how learning works and strive to help students learn "how to learn" skills.

4. Successful teachers help students learn to memorize some aspects of the content so that necessary basics are learned to the level of automaticity.
5. Successful teachers know that motivating students is part of their job.
6. Successful teachers accept students who enter the room, meet them at their developmental and cognitive levels, and then lead them to higher levels of learning.

Chapter Three

Organize and Manage the Classroom

> The successful teacher organizes time, space, students, and materials.

A teacher with ten years of experience said that she had changed schools three times because she was looking for "better students." "You know what I mean," she added, "students who know how to behave." If this teacher had said this line in a job interview, I would NEVER have hired her. She was admitting her own lack of success. She had never learned how to become established in a classroom and how to manage student behavior.

Truly successful teachers know that they have to teach students how to be students whether they are teaching first grade or sophomore English. Today's students do not walk into classrooms, sit down, get their materials ready, and then say, "Please, teach me." Oh no, they do not! Successful teachers know that they have to master classroom organization and management to survive. Success follows basic survival.

Dr. Harry K. Wong and Rosemary T. Wong (2009), considered leaders in the field of classroom management, have defined classroom management to be "all of the things a teacher does to organize students, space, time, and materials so student learning can take place" (p. 83). The Wongs are also famous for the line "What you do on the first days of school will determine your success or failure for the rest of the school year" (2009, p. 3).

The last time I did an online search for "classroom management and discipline," I got one and a half million hits. A lot has been written about how to manage a classroom, how to get students to be quiet, how to make rules and consequences that work, and every other possible topic associated with managing the classroom. Let's narrow this huge field to four doable steps:

1. Organize the room
2. Create procedures and routines
3. Build a classroom management plan and use it
4. Have meaningful, relevant, and rigorous instruction

ORGANIZE THE ROOM

As soon as you are hired, ask when you can work in your room. If you are an experienced teacher, decide how much time you need to get your room up and ready for students. Many, many things must be done before the first day of school. Yes, this will take time away from your summer vacation, and no, you won't be paid for these days in your classroom. But the early effort will make the school year start smoothly.

Minkel (2017) wrote that it is important to visualize what you want your room to look like and then make your dream room happen. His four areas include:

1. Imagine student movement in and out of the room. Can students get to their seats and move to the other areas of the room when needed?
2. Make all material accessible. Think like a student about getting math manipulatives, glue sticks, or pencils.
3. Visualize the walls of the classroom as areas for teaching resources, posters, and student work.
4. Think about the books needed in your room. Is your class library filled with books that are appropriate for your students?

Minkel reminds readers that "the only way out is through" and careful thought about the work of getting the classroom ready is what gets teachers through the beginning—and the rest—of the year.

Do I Assign Seats?

Many theorists say no. It is their belief that having students choose their seats emphasizes good decision making (Kronowitz, 2008). In a perfect world, where students come to school ready to learn, this might just work. In the real world, successful teachers assign seats before the first day of school and get students seated and working quickly. "Don't make finding one's seat on the first day of school a frustrating treasure hunt" (Wong & Wong, 2009). Assign seats!

And how should seats be arranged? The research on classroom management is strikingly clear. At the beginning of the year, students should all be seated to face the front. That's right—having rows of seats facing the front is the foremost method for good classroom management. It's a starting place.

Once students learn how the classroom is managed, of course, you will have group work and students working at tables, but students need to face the front either in rows or in a modified theater-style arrangement when school starts.

Students need desks, by the way. In elementary school, students need some personal space. They are much better at getting themselves organized if they have a place for their stuff. I have observed in dozens of elementary schools where students were seated at tables, with no room for their belongings. They had to drape huge backpacks over the backs of their chairs or, worse yet, had to put their materials in recycled grocery bags that were hung over the backs of chairs.

True story: A teacher was hired to begin work in January after an ineffective teacher retired. The teacher was warned that "not much learning took place in the fall." The teacher looked at the room several days before the semester was to begin and then went to the principal. "May I clean out the room, and more importantly, may I have desks for my students?" Surprised, the principal said, "Well, yes, to both questions. We have desks from about 15 years ago when students sat in rows. Are you sure you want them? Everybody here uses tables so that students can work together."

The new hire replied, "My decision to use desks is research based. Every student has to see the front of the room where the screen is. If students face each other, they do talk, but they talk all the time, and about everything but their subjects. I have to turn this class around and teach them a year's worth of material in a semester, and I need to get their attention from the first minute of each day."

The desks were brought in to replace the tables. The walls were cleaned, and fresh materials were posted. (It took the teacher three whole days and some help from others to do this.) There were clear paths to everything in the room. On the first day of the semester, the new teacher stood at the doorway and greeted students. "Your name is on your new desk. Please go directly there, sit down, and read what's on the screen. Start the assignment on the screen as everyone is entering. I will check your work as class starts. It's going to be a great new year." It was.

Did this teacher do group work? Yes, when appropriate, but he didn't do group work until his students learned the procedures for being fourth-grade students. His students learned, and both he and his students achieved success.

20 Things to Do before the First Day of School

1. Find your room. Count the desks. Compare the number of desks to the number of students on your roster. Have enough desks and one or two extra ones in case the roster is not correct.
2. Arrange the desks so that all students are facing the front. Rows are a good thing.

3. Walk around the room. Can students get to seats easily? Are there clear paths around the room?
4. Walk to the back of the room. Can you see the screen clearly?
5. Where will you store your purse, cell phone, or anything of value? You need a locked drawer if you are going to leave anything of value in the room.
6. Know the building. Where are the student restrooms? Emergency exits? How does a student request permission for restroom use?
7. Know at least one colleague well enough to run across the hall and ask him or her a question. You will have questions.
8. Learn the basic school policies before the first day. What do you do when a student is late? How do you turn in attendance on the computer program, and when is attendance due?
9. How does lunch work for students? For you?
10. How will students leave the room for transportation home?
11. Test the technology. Can you pull up online programs needed? Showing a PowerPoint of who you are and of the classroom procedures and rules is a great first-day lesson.
12. Plan for an entrance table. This is a table where students pick up materials needed for the class. (Think about handouts, workbooks, a card with the laptop password of the week, etc.)
13. Hang your classroom management poster on the wall. It should have three to five rules and consequences and some positive reinforcements.
14. Make bulletin boards with welcoming signs, learning materials, and the emergency routines.
15. Post the bell schedule. Depending on the grade you teach and the culture of the school, you may be able to create a welcome sign with students' names. (Ask first. In many schools, this is not done because of confidentiality issues.)
16. Make sure your name and the number of the room are clearly visible so that students can find your room.
17. Become acquainted with the custodian for your hallway and the support staff members (secretaries). Know their names and be nice to them!
18. Locate your class's textbooks, laptops, and other materials. Plan where to store them in your room so they are accessible.
19. Gather extra supplies. They might include a first aid kit, tissues, hand lotion, and safety pins.
20. Create a letter (paper or electronic) to send to parents and students before the first day of class. This letter should be very welcoming in tone and serve as an introduction to you and your qualifications to teach. (For more ideas, see, for example, Clement, 2003.)

The Wongs (2009) wrote that effective teachers "have the room ready, have the materials ready, and have themselves ready" (p. 89). Just how do teachers get themselves ready for a new school year? Do they psych up or meditate or strive to find their Zen? Although there are as many different ways to get yourself ready for the first day of school as there are teachers, here are a few suggestions:

1. Sleep. A well-rested teacher can think more clearly than an exhausted one.
2. Eat. A healthy diet helps everyone. Consider packing a lunch instead of hitting the high-carb student lunch line or the high-sugar snack machine.
3. Dress professionally. Each school has its own norms for how teachers dress. Although jeans and polo shirts are appropriate for many teachers, they are not appropriate apparel in all schools. Low-cut tops and short skirts are never appropriate for female teachers, nor are skin-tight pants for males. It is truly embarrassing when a teacher is sent home by the principal to change clothes, and yes, it happens frequently.
4. Keep an extra white T-shirt in your room for yourself because schools can be messy places or you might just spill coffee. An extra sweater or jacket is a good idea too because schools can get cold.
5. Practice your commute to school before the first day but at a time that you would normally leave. Teachers cannot be late!
6. Plan for your own stress management. As a new teacher, I walked to and from work, and that walk was my stress management. Other people plan to go to the gym or run after school.
7. Create your professional support network. How will you keep in touch with other teachers? Consider Kappa Delta Pi's online social network. It works a little like Facebook, but it's password protected and professional in nature. (Go to kdp.org and look for kdpglobal. Parts of the site are open to members only, and other parts are free to all.) *Do not* use Facebook or a public blog to complain about students, administrators, or colleagues.
8. Enlist your family's support for your teaching job. Teaching is considered a family-friendly profession, and your family needs to understand that you will work extra hours at home.

Finally, What to Do ON the First Day

Remember that you get only one chance to make a good first impression. The first day is important. You should arrive early and be ready for the students' arrival. Check your mailbox or your inbox to see whether there are any last-minute instructions for teachers from the principal. As much as you may like coffee, finish it and your breakfast before the students arrive.

Stand at the door and greet students. Younger students will need much help to find their seats. Older students can be handed a card with the row and seat number of their seat. A seating chart can be posted on the screen so that students know where to sit. As students arrive, direct them to read the board and start an assignment. The assignments may already be on their desks. This can work for all grade and subject levels.

Introduce yourself at the start of the day or start of each class that enters the room. Your introduction can include:

- Where you went to college
- A bit about your family or pets
- What you did over the summer
- What you like to teach, and what you are excited about for the upcoming year

Next, it can be good to introduce your first procedure—how to talk and listen in class. Describe the procedure and then use the procedure for students to introduce themselves. For students who can already write independently and for all upper elementary, middle, and high school students, an interest inventory is a great first-day assignment. Before distributing the assignment, teach how papers are distributed and how names must be written on papers. Then, the interest inventory is the practice of those procedures.

What is an interest inventory? It's a quick survey of students' interests and backgrounds in the subject area of your class. Although a survey for second-graders may look quite different than one for students in the second year of high school, here are some sample questions:

1. The best book I have ever read is . . .
2. My favorite movie is . . .
3. My favorite TV show is . . .
4. In my free time, I like to . . .
5. The subject that I may be best at is . . .

Then, there should be some content material questions. Examples follow:

1. Write a short paragraph about your summer. (This reveals their writing skills.)
2. Solve the following three math problems and show your work.
3. Write two things you have learned in the past about World War I.

Although the first few weeks of school should be about teaching procedures, routines, and the rules for the classroom, a successful teacher intersperses the lessons of how the class will run with content lessons. Show a demonstration of a science lesson to wow the students about science, or give a very interesting 10-minute lecture about geography to pique students' interest about your social studies class. Reading a fun book is always a good first-day activity in elementary classes.

PROCEDURES AND ROUTINES

Every classroom needs procedures and routines because there are myriads of movements and activities going on in that room. Just as you visualized how to set up your classroom for the first day of school, visualize what students will do in the room. What procedures are needed?

1. How to enter the classroom and put away book bags, backpacks, and outerwear
2. How to pick up necessary materials—handouts, textbooks, calculators, laptops
3. What to do as the class starts—announcements, pledge, lunch count
4. What to do when one is late
5. What to do when one needs to use the restroom
6. How to find out what we are doing today
7. How to turn in a paper
8. How to ask a question
9. How to find out what the assignment was when one misses a class
10. How to get extra help
11. How to get to lunch
12. How to leave the building and get transportation home
13. How the teacher will quiet the class and get attention
14. How to move to stations or anywhere in the room
15. What the emergency procedures are
16. What to do when an announcement is made from the office
17. How to respectfully address the teacher and other students
18. What the test-taking procedures are
19. How to take a test when one was missed
20. What the special procedures for labs are

Once you decide on a procedure, how will you teach it to students? You will need to explain it and then model it for students, have them practice, and reinforce that procedure until it becomes a routine. For seven-year-olds to seventeen-year-olds, practice is important. The authors of the Responsive

Classroom (2015) series of books wrote that "For students to do well from the start, a sense of order and predictability in daily school life is critical" (p. 3).

When visual reminders accompany the explanations, students remember the procedures better. Post the procedures around the room. When starting a new activity, show the procedure on the screen and narrate what students are supposed to do. Of course, you don't have to rehearse every procedure the first week of class, just the most important ones needed to make the classroom run smoothly. You will introduce procedures in advance of an assembly when one is announced and approaching.

Academic procedures are critically important. How does one head a paper to be turned in to the teacher? How does one submit an assignment electronically? What is the procedure for taking a test? Many teachers have found that on the days of the standardized tests, students really can concentrate for longer lengths of time and sit quietly when finished. Why? Their teachers have taught and rehearsed procedures and have high expectations that the students must follow the procedures. Some teachers even say, "It's state law that you do this on the day of the standardized test." With enough practice and the strength of expectation, every day can yield high results.

RULES AND CONSEQUENCES

I have observed student teachers in hundreds of classrooms in two states. My student teachers often go in to classrooms and report that it's hard to get students to do what they should be doing because there are no rules in the classroom. No rules? Not even for crazy sixth-graders? No wonder the students aren't listening or behaving. Sometimes, the student teachers report that the teacher has guidelines posted, such as "be nice" or "be respectful," but no actual rules.

For some veteran teachers, whose reputations of being no-nonsense teachers precede them, maybe all they need is a few guidelines. However, even for these teachers, for good management, and to meet legal guidelines, there should be rules with consequences posted. For all teachers, posted rules with consequences are a preventive measure. Posted rules protect the teacher and make invisible expectations visible.

Long known for their work with assertive discipline, Lee and Marlene Canter (1993) advocate that all teachers be proactive, not reactive. Being proactive means that a teacher knows what to do when a student talks back rudely, provokes peers, or throws a desk. A reactive teacher does not have a plan in place for dealing with infractions, and when a misbehavior occurs, he or she reacts with anger.

Although the Canters' work (1993) stresses building trust with students, establishing positive relationships, and teaching appropriate behavior, they also place utmost importance on a management/discipline plan for all classrooms. What should be on a management plan? Rules with consequences and positive reinforcements. The wording could be rules with corrective actions and supportive feedback (Canter & Canter, 2001). Some educators have said that the word *rules* is too harsh a word and that *guidelines* is a softer word. Really? In a world with school shootings and violent crimes, *rules* seems to be quite an appropriate word, but each teacher should decide based on the culture of the school where he or she teaches.

A rule should be simple and straightforward. Three to five rules work best, as follows:

1. Keep hands, feet, and objects to yourself.
2. Follow all directions.
3. Use only positive language.
4. Be where you are supposed to be in the classroom.
5. Leave your seat/the room only with permission.

These rules fit first grade through the senior year of high school. Each rule covers quite a bit. There is no need for a rule such as "no throwing" because that is covered by rule number one. One could create a rule such as "no swearing, insults, or putdowns," but rule three covers that. Of course, the teacher has to teach what positive language is to each grade level. When I was growing up, we couldn't say *crap* in our household without getting in trouble. Now, many teachers would accept *crap* as a much better four-letter word than many other harsher ones.

A rule should be general enough that it can be enforced at all times during the class and throughout the day. Having a rule such as "no talking" makes no sense because you need students to talk in your classes. Many teachers want a rule for materials—"bring all materials and a pen or pencil to class." This is not a good rule because your consequences will include notifying parents and sending students to the office. No teacher should be sending students to the office for not having a pencil. The pencil issue can be solved in other ways.

The rules have to be posted in the room. They have to be taught and reviewed periodically. The rules must fit within the school's norms for rules. As Kronowitz (2008) wrote, "Don't reinvent the wheel. . . . Ask colleagues what their rules are and how they abide by the generic and district rules" (p. 76). Sending a letter home on the first day of school will inform parents of the rules. The rules are just a third of a management/discipline plan. The positives and the consequences complete the plan.

Consequences of Breaking a Rule

Years ago, teachers and school administrators used the term *punishment* when referring to how to deal with students who broke rules. *Punishment* sounds like sending students to prison for a crime, so *consequences* has become the word used. The Canters (1993) use corrective actions in their management plan. The point of consequences is to help students learn proper behavior and use it consistently.

Successful teachers are very cautious when talking to parents about correcting student behavior. They are assertive but positive, using a line such as "Your student received the correction to his behavior for him to learn better. It is your student's success that is of utmost concern."

What are sample corrections? They can include:

- A verbal warning
- A written warning
- A one-minute personal conference with the teacher after class
- A few minutes separated from the class at the side of the room where they can still hear instruction of content material
- A detention after school if this is part of the school policy
- A think sheet on which the student writes what he or she did and what he or she will do differently in the future
- A parent contact—e-mail or phone call
- An office referral, depending on the amount of backup provided by the school
- Last to leave the room

When planning corrective actions/consequences, it is important to remember what *not* to do. Teachers never humiliate students publicly with negative comments. Corrections cannot be physically or psychologically hurtful. We don't have students do push-ups for talking too much. Withholding recess may make the situation worse because students need to run around and burn off energy. We do not touch students. When a student's behavior is so difficult that a restraint is needed, get backup help from the office.

Positive Reinforcements

Once called rewards, we are striving not to reward students for each and every little behavior now. Rather, when students do behave, our classroom management plan may have some positive reinforcement or feedback for students. In a perfect world, the positive outcome for correct behavior is a happy classroom. What else might students want as positive reinforcement?

- Positive comments to the student

- Earning a few minutes of talk time at the end of a class
- Earning some time for free reading or a game
- Earning extra recess time
- Positive call, email, or note home to parents
- Select your own seat for the day
- Read in the reader's chair

You will notice that candy, popcorn, and ice cream are not on this list. Today's students are bombarded with sweets and treats in schools, and teachers should strive not to reward with food. How about stickers? Although better than food, stickers, tickets for prizes, and other tangible rewards can easily be overused. It takes a strong teacher to buck the system and not reinforce every little action with something, but in the long run, students will be better off without the candy and the tangibles. A positive word and a thumbs up, combined with a smile, can go a long way with a third-grade student or a junior in high school.

What does the final classroom management plan look like? The rules are stated clearly as are the consequences and positives. The consequences have a hierarchy because a teacher shouldn't "throw the book" at a student for a minor infraction but rather warn the student to get him or her back on track. After the first warning, if the behavior continues, then the consequences mount.

A severe clause is necessary for any plan because sometimes students' behavior may become violent and put the student or others at risk for harm. Each school should have a plan for supporting the teacher with a severe student behavioral issue.

MANAGEMENT PLAN FOR ELEMENTARY AND MIDDLE SCHOOL

Classroom Rules

1. Keep hands, feet, and objects to yourself.
2. Follow all directions.
3. Use only positive language.
4. Be where you are supposed to be in the classroom.
5. Leave the room only with permission.

Consequences/Corrective Actions

1. Verbal warning; written warning
2. Five minutes at the side of the room for time-out

3. Loss of privilege time/free time
4. Parent contact
5. Office referral

Positives

1. Additional privilege time/free time for reading
2. Choice of seat for an hour
3. Positive parent contact
4. A "You did great today" card

Severe Clause

For a severe misbehavior that puts the student or others at risk, the resource officer and office administrators will remove the student and apply the school rules.

MANAGEMENT PLAN FOR HIGH SCHOOL

Classroom Rules

1. Keep hands, feet, and objects to yourself.
2. Follow all directions.
3. Use only positive language.
4. Be where you are supposed to be in the classroom.
5. Leave the room only with permission.

Consequences

1. Teacher warning—verbal or written
2. 10 minutes at the side of the room, writing a think sheet
3. Serve a 30-minute detention after school per the school plan
4. Parent contact
5. Office referral

Positives

1. Free time at the end of class for checking messages (tablet or phone)
2. Positive parent contact
3. Free ticket to a school event earned over time

Severe Clause

> For a severe misbehavior that puts the student or others at risk, the resource officer and office administrators will remove the student and apply the school rules.

The management/discipline plan should be posted in the room, and students and parents need a copy. The principal also needs a copy. In today's world, parents and their attorney may come to school to contest a detention or other consequence. If students and parents were not informed about consequences, the likelihood of getting their support or legal support is very limited.

What Does a Teacher Do When the Plan Isn't Enough?

Many students have emotional and psychological issues that affect their behavior at school. Students on prescription drugs, as well as students who abuse alcohol and drugs, may have significant behavior issues. What are some steps for working with students with significant issues?

1. For some students, an individual behavior management plan works well. Each student will have his or her own plan, with modified and generally more specific rules and consequences. Students identified as exceptional education/special education will already have an individualized education plan (IEP) that stipulates their behavior guidelines and consequences.
2. Schools need psychologists on staff to work with teachers for certain students. The use of applied behavioral analysis (ABA) is becoming more prevalent in schools. In ABA, a trained specialist observes a student, diagnoses issues, plans an intervention, helps to implement the intervention, and then assesses the results of the intervention on the student's behavior. It takes time and trained specialists to implement this help for a student.
3. Enlist the support of the special education teachers, school counselors, and administrators when trying to improve a student's behavior. Have parent conferences with the counselor or administrator present.
4. Document every incident objectively and share documentation with special education teachers, counselors, and administrators.
5. For extreme cases, work with your professional association to get needed backup help or to get students out of your classroom and in to an alternative situation. You do not have to put up with continual behavioral issues that disrupt your classroom.
6. Follow the school's protocol for removal of students from classrooms to an alternative setting.

ENGAGE STUDENTS IN MEANINGFUL, RELEVANT, AND RIGOROUS INSTRUCTION

Several years ago, I was observing in a high school classroom. Toward the end of the lesson, a student pulled out his tablet and began watching a movie. At the end of class, I asked him about the movie. He said that there was so much downtime in his classes that he could generally watch an entire movie each day in school. How could a student have 90 to 120 minutes of downtime in a school setting?

While teaching one of my college courses in management, I posed the question to student teachers, "How do we keep students on task?" A student teacher replied, "Have a task." At first, I thought she was being sarcastic, but she said that her cooperating teacher never had anything for the students to do when the bell rang. It took her teacher 20 minutes to figure out what each class should do that hour, and by then, the students were not behaving and didn't want to settle down for any meaningful learning. Obviously, that student teacher was moved to another placement where she could see best practice in teaching.

Both of these examples point to the fact that sometimes teachers create their students' behavior issues. Although the student who watched movies wasn't causing any overt discipline problems, he wasn't learning the content material either. Other students who didn't have tablets with movies on them might cause issues out of sheer boredom.

In the second example, a teacher who has nothing for students to do will have behavioral issues arise. She will say that her students are noisy and don't work, but the truth is that she didn't take charge and organize the learning.

Making Learning Challenging

The trick is to make learning challenging but not so much so that students are overly frustrated because frustrated students misbehave too. It is hitting Vygotsky's Zone of Proximal Development (ZPD) as discussed in educational psychology (Woolfolk, 2016).

Many principals observe teachers and want to see student engagement "bell to bell." This is a good thing. There is so much to learn that students shouldn't have a lot of downtime in their classrooms. Some students actually tell their parents that they got in trouble because nothing was going on in their classroom. Have something going on—preferably learning!

Perhaps Breaux and Whitaker (2010) said it best:

> Great teachers teach with a sense of urgency. They reel their students in with "teasers" and leave them wanting more, wondering what mysteries will be

uncovered in tomorrow's lesson. They are storytellers, actors, salespeople, and infomercials all rolled into one! (p. 98)

THE FOUR STEPS OF CLASSROOM MANAGEMENT

1. Organize the room.

   - Create clear paths for student entrance and exit.
   - Have students facing front to start the school year.
   - Make sure that students have personal space.
   - Plan for places for students to keep belongings and supplies.

2. Create procedures that become routines.

   - Everything needs a procedure—how to sharpen pencils, how to turn in papers, how to return a laptop.
   - Teach and practice the procedures until they become routines.
   - Make visuals/posters of procedures and refer to them.
   - Reteach procedures on Mondays and special event days, such as Halloween or homecoming.

3. Make a classroom management plan and use it.

   - The plan needs three to five rules, consequences, and positive reinforcements.
   - Post the plan in your room, and give parents and the principal a copy.
   - Have a severe clause in the plan for emergency situations.
   - Use the plan.

4. Have engaging, meaningful, relevant, and rigorous instruction.

   - Use your lesson plans.
   - Keep students busy bell to bell.

KEYS FOR SUCCESS

1. Successful teachers organize their classrooms before the first day of school.
2. Successful teachers have classrooms where students can face the front, get materials easily, and have personal space for their belongings.

3. Successful teachers plan procedures for everything—from how to enter the room to how to sharpen a pencil.
4. Successful teachers' procedures are taught until they are routines. Routines are not ruts but ways to keep students organized.
5. Successful teachers have management/discipline plans with rules, consequences, and positives. They teach their plans as would the curriculum.
6. Successful teachers know when to get backup help.
7. Successful teachers plan to keep students busy and learning.

Chapter Four

Plan for Teaching

Successful teachers know that failing to plan is planning to fail.

What is the most common reason that teachers plan? They are terrified of standing up in front of students with nothing to do! This may not be the best reason to plan, but fear can be a motivator. We plan because there is so much to teach students and there is more to teach than there is ever enough time to do so. When it comes to planning, teachers must first know what to teach and then know how to organize what they teach. The first involves knowledge of the curriculum, and the second involves learning how to divide the curriculum into manageable lessons, units, and semesters.

CURRICULUM IS WHAT WE TEACH

Put succinctly, curriculum is what is taught in the schools. Some say that curriculum is a plan for learning. It's a road map or a set of guidelines. What are the big issues of curriculum? In other words, what are schools for?

The Five Big Pillars of Curriculum

Schools exist and have a curriculum to do several things. The big picture of curriculum includes five areas:

1. Teaching students to be citizens
2. Preparing students to be workers
3. Helping students to self-actualize
4. Keeping knowledge alive; having students learn for the sake of learning

5. Promoting sustainable development of the world's environment, societies, and economies

In other words, the curriculum of the schools is designed on two basic premises:

1. To meet the needs of society (creation of workers and citizens, keeping knowledge alive, sustainable development)
2. To meet the needs of the individual (learning for the sake of learning, self-actualization)

The curriculum should teach students to be good citizens. In the United States, our schools are a way to promote democracy. Our schools teach students the value of voting, of participating in a democracy, and of the responsibilities that citizens have. If the schools fail at this mission, what might be the repercussions? The results might be disastrous.

How do teachers teach the curriculum of citizenship? In lower elementary grades, teachers teach who the president is; what certain holidays are for; and the concepts of nation, state, and community. Social studies have long been the content area for the teaching of citizenship. In high school history classes, students hone their knowledge of our country and other countries in the world.

The curriculum of the schools prepares students to be good workers because society needs good workers. On the practical level, teachers teach reading, writing, and mathematics because workers need to know how to read, write, and perform math. Historically, most high schools had a vocational track so that students would get specific training for area businesses while in high school. The businesses sometimes supplied resources and guest teachers to ensure that the students were learning the specific skills needed. Upon graduation, the best students were hired by businesses in the community.

The hidden/informal curriculum of the schools also teaches students to be good workers. Schools promote attendance and prompt arrival, with penalties for students who don't attend on time or don't attend at all. Attendance and punctuality are traits needed by employers.

Today's employers need workers who are problem solvers and team players, and these two traits have worked their way into the curriculum of the schools. Every teacher has heard that he or she is supposed to be producing "lifelong learners" and students who can problem solve. The use of cooperative learning is designed to create workers who can work on teams.

When corporations donate to schools, their generosity is lauded, but their gifts may be self-serving. Big businesses want better schools so that their plants can be staffed by better prepared workers—saving them millions of dollars in training.

It is the value of student self-actualization that may be a fuzzier area of the curriculum. How can a school help each student "to find himself or herself" and to find meaning in life? How do teachers go about teaching to this pillar of curriculum? When a teacher of literature has students discuss a book and look at the protagonist's life, that teacher may be meeting this curricular goal. The teacher may point out that the main character had a sad life because of one bad decision. This leads students to think about their own lives and to begin the self-actualization process.

Most schools offer guidance counseling to help students learn to make good choices in life. Guidance sessions might include how to choose a college, how to find a career, or how to manage money. Classes in life skills also fit the self-actualization portion of the curriculum.

How many of you have studied Latin? Should everyone study Latin and a modern language? These curricular decisions are made based on the goal of keeping knowledge alive and having students learn for the sake of learning. Some might argue that learning Latin is a necessary part of the curriculum for students to see how language works and grammar is built. Others argue that a modern foreign language course will meet the same purposes and give students a way to communicate in other countries. Just how much classical knowledge is needed?

Lastly, but perhaps most importantly, sustainability has become a part of the curriculum. First, students started learning about saving the planet with recycling and conservation of resources, but sustainable development is so much more than just the physical environment. Although sustaining the physical environment is critically important, education for sustainable development (ESD) includes learning how to sustain a nation's society and its economy.

How do teachers do this? Elementary teachers begin with teaching the concepts of environment, society, and economy. Many elementary classrooms use token economies for students to learn the value of money. High school students study economics as a semester course. Having recycling bins throughout a school teaches recycling. Involving the students in an activity to sustain a preferred school activity, such as homecoming or the fall festival, also teaches the concept of sustainability.

Do teachers get up in the morning, look in the mirror, and say to themselves, "Today, I am going to teach my students to be good citizens, workers, and learners of the classics and sustainability, all while helping them to self-actualize?" I doubt that teachers do this, but in the big picture of schooling, this is what we do. On the practical side, most teachers do plan to meet national, state, district, and school curriculum guidelines.

The Common Core Curriculum

For eighteen years, I taught a graduate course in curriculum theory. No matter which textbook I used, there was always a debate about whether the United States needed a national curriculum like some other countries have. Most theorists wrote that the United States wouldn't move to a national curriculum because of our long history of local control of schools. Others postured that the diversity of our nation was simply too great for one national curriculum.

Standards for curriculum are different than a prescribed national or state curriculum. Professional associations were the first groups to adopt curriculum standards. In 1989, the first standards were released for mathematics education by the National Council of Teachers of Mathematics (www.nctm.org/). These standards were voluntary guidelines for those teaching mathematics. Other professional organizations followed suit and published standards throughout the 1990s.

The Common Core State Standards (CCSS) were developed by the Council of Chief School Administrators (CCSSO) and the National Governors Association Center for Best Practices (Carjuzaa & Kellough, 2017) with the input of many professional education organizations. They were first released for public comment in 2010, and then each state decided on adoption of the standards. The standards are not a curriculum because they do not state what must be taught but rather identify "the essential elements of a basic core of subject knowledge that all students should acquire (Carjuzaa & Kellough, 2017, p. 32). Go to www.corestandards.org/about-the-standards/ for more information.

In states where the CCSS are adopted, and that is most states, teachers start their planning of what to teach with the standards. Some states may add to the standards or adopt only some of them. Districts may plan a curriculum that exceeds the CCSS and the state's standards. Does this sound complicated? Yes and no. Standards help guide teachers in their work. Standards should help to eliminate gaps in student learning and minimize repetition of topics.

In most schools, curriculum directors help teachers to understand all the standards and plan the year's curriculum accordingly. Textbooks are published according to the standards, and teachers who use an up-to-date textbook have much of the organization of the year's work done for them by the books used. Using the standards is similar to using a road map—you need to know where you are going before you decide which road to take.

PLANNING WHAT TO TEACH

Understanding by Design

As a first-year teacher, I went into the teacher's lounge to eat my lunch and announced that I was indeed going to get to the end of the book by the end of the school year. A much wiser teacher asked me, "Are the students going to get to the end of the book, or just you?" I was intent on content coverage and keeping the students busy with activities to try to end the year without any major discipline problems. I didn't know at the time that I committed two educational planning sins.

The phrases "start with the end in mind" and "backward by design" have become commonplace in educational vocabulary. The history behind these phrases is found with Wiggins and McTighe's (2000) work on understanding by design (UbD). These authors have long stressed that there are "twin sins of typical instructional design in schools: activity-focused teaching and coverage-focused teaching" (p. 3).

Think about your own teaching. Do you start planning by asking yourself how you will keep students busy doing things to fill up the hours (activity based), or do you look at some curriculum guide and the textbook and ask yourself how long it will take to cover the material (coverage focused)? It's what teachers have done for ages. And quite frankly, learning can result from doing this, so it may not necessarily be a big sin.

Wiggins and McTighe (2000) stress that "teachers are designers" (p. 13). Teachers craft learning experiences. They remind teachers that by planning the learning experiences with the end in mind, lessons and units have greater effect. Their three stages of backward design include:

1. Identify desired results
2. Determine acceptable evidence of learning
3. Plan learning experiences and instruction (Wiggins & McTighe, 2000, p. 18)

These steps are helpful as you plan lessons and units, mapping out what you will teach over the course of the semester and year. I am reminded of what a veteran teacher once said in a speech about her teaching career. Her words were "Cute has to count." She meant that although teachers, especially elementary teachers, want to have cute, fun activities frequently, those activities should always be directed at a learning goal.

Planning a Lesson

A lesson can be as short as a few minutes or as long as a couple of hours. The lesson is the building block for teaching. In colleges of teacher education, students are taught to write extensive plans, some of which might be five pages long to teach 35 minutes. In the real world, an experienced teacher may be able to write a few reminders in a two-inch square and teach a great lesson from just those reminders. What makes a good plan?

1. Start with the standards. What CCSS does this lesson cover?
2. Think about what the student must know or be able to do as the result of the lesson. Called the objective in most districts, this might also be called a learning target. It's the end result in backward design/understanding by design.
3. Think about what you, the teacher, must do to help the student reach the lesson's objective. This is a teacher goal.
4. What methods, strategies, and presentations will be used to convey the new material?
5. How will students engage with the content material (practice, draw, problem solve, debate, answer questions, discuss, etc.)?
6. How much time is needed for teacher presentation of material and for student engagement/practice with material?
7. How will you build assessment into the lesson? How will you know whether students have mastered the objective/learning target?
8. How will you review or close the lesson?
9. What do you need to teach (materials, technology, etc.)?

A TEN-STEP LESSON PLAN—ANY SUBJECT OR GRADE LEVEL

1. Standard:
2. Objective(s): The student will (TSW) ...
3. Goal for the teacher: The teacher will (TTW) ...
4. Step-by-step procedures for teaching:

    TTW ... (present, read, demonstrate, show, model)
    TTW ... (show a website, use the Smart Board, show a video clip)

5. Steps for student engagement:

    TSW ... (read, write, listen, solve, practice)
    ***Steps 4 and 5 should be interspersed in short intervals.

6. Assessment of learning is ongoing:

    TSW answer questions, solve problems, complete a written exercise

7. TTW conclude the lesson:

    Be explicit about what students learned and why they need the content material.

    Students may make the conclusion, making summaries of what they learned.

8. Resources needed
9. Accommodations for exceptional learners
10. Teacher reflection/self-evaluation of the lesson

Although the ten-step plan covers everything thoroughly, when teaching in a very busy, hectic elementary, middle, or high school, can you remember 10 steps? I have condensed and simplified planning into four steps. Not only is this very doable, but teachers can write a four-step plan on a notecard and carry it around while teaching. Try it!

A FOUR-STEP LESSON PLAN

1. Focus: The teacher starts the lesson by catching the students' attention. A review or preview sets the tone to meet curriculum standards and attain student objectives and the teacher's goals.
2. Presentation of new material: TTW explain, model, demonstrate, read, and teach with a variety of methods and strategies. (Think about teaching in short bursts to hold student attention.)
3. Application of material: TSW practice material independently and in groups. (This step is interspersed with step 2, and the teacher provides guidance and feedback to students. Assessment is ongoing.)
4. Review, conclusion, assessments: TTW make the learning explicit while also assessing student learning and what to do next. Good questions to ask students include "What is the most important thing you learned in this lesson?" and "What is still unclear or confusing from today's lesson?"

With this plan, some of the steps are automatic—such as resources and accommodations for children with exceptionalities. The teacher still needs to plan well for those things, but thinking in terms of four steps tends to simplify the process.

TEMPLATE FOR THE EASIEST LESSON PLAN EVER

What are my goals for this lesson (present, introduce, review, demonstrate)?

Objective: What will the students know or be able to do at the end of the lesson?

TSW:

Standard(s) met:

1. Focus/introduction
2. Presentation of new material
3. Application of material
4. Review and assessment

Reminders of what I need to get ready for teaching (materials, technology)
Reminders of who needs special attention/help/differentiation

Another way to think about lesson planning is to envision what you, the teacher, will be doing and what students will be doing for each step you do. A visual for this is shown in figure 4.1.

Writing Objectives

I remember learning how to teach in college methods courses. Students wrote lengthy objectives that read as follows:

- Given a map of the United States, the student will identify the states that made up the confederacy in the Civil War, with 85 percent accuracy.
- Given regular –ar, –er, and –ir verbs in Spanish, the student will conjugate the verbs in present tense with 95 percent accuracy.

Each objective had to be measurable, with some background, and had to include action verbs. We did not say *understand* or *appreciate* in objectives because those verbs are just not measurable.

Then, as a first-year teacher, my goals for student objectives were written differently:

- Do exercises on page 17.
- Read the dialogues for chapter 2.
- Complete the sentences on page 41.

There was a bit of a disconnect between theory and practice here. Student teachers and beginning teachers need to write out more detailed objectives to ensure coverage of content and to know what to assess. More experienced teachers know the curriculum so well that their goals and the students' objectives are second nature. In this age of teacher accountability, most teachers are required not only to write out standards, goals, and objectives but also to

Plan for Teaching 53

The Lesson	The teacher will...	The students will...
1. Focus/hook	TTW review, preview material	TSW listen, list, answer
2. Lesson Purpose	TTW share standard/objective	TSW read or make an essential question in student language
3. Visuals and Materials	TTW need	TSW need
4. Presentation of Material	TTW show, lecture, model, use technology	TSW listen, take notes, use technology
5. Application	TTW monitor and give feedback	TWS practice, share answers, work in groups
6. Assessment	Ongoing, informal assessment; performance assessments	Student self-assessment; summative assessments
7. Extension of learning	TTW plan accommodations, homework	TSW practice

Figure 4.1.

post them in their classrooms and direct students explicitly to those statements.

A Word about Words

Education is filled with words with different meanings in different classrooms and schools around the country. What one district may call goals another district calls objectives. I have always thought of the goal as what the teacher wants to accomplish and the objective as what the student will know or do, but other educators have different definitions. The phrase "learning targets" is now in vogue in some education programs. A lesson can be called a learning segment.

When a teacher gets a job, he or she must learn new vocabulary for planning and assessment. There will always be changes. I was teaching about graphic organizers in a graduate class, and a practicing teacher said that they didn't use them in her school. She went on to explain in detail about some kind of specific mind map that had to be in a square and have writing on the edges. "Oh yes, I've seen those," I said. "It's just another kind of visual like a graphic organizer." "Oh no," she practically shouted. "It's not a visual or a graphic organizer; it's a mind map, and every teacher at my school must make one for every lesson."

This same teacher, who was studying to become a principal, went on to tell the class that every teacher had to use the same lesson plan and that the plan was the only one sanctioned by the state. She couldn't wrap her head around the idea that lesson plans could look different for different teachers, different grade levels, and different subjects. She wouldn't even accept that her mind map could fit into a general category of a visual aid. Her training had been that there was one way to do each step of teaching, and that's what she had to do. By the way, our state has no official lesson plan and never has!

Sadly, when this woman becomes a principal, she will have the strictest of guidelines for everything in the school. Each teacher will have to use one plan, one mind map, and who knows what else will be prescribed for the teachers. As a teacher, you need flexibility in your workplace. Take the lesson plans you were taught in your training, compare them to the ones in this chapter, and make your own. When you take ownership of planning, the other parts of teaching fall right into place.

Essential Questions

Many teachers say, "We teach to the standards" and "Our classrooms are standards driven." Some administrators go in to teachers' classrooms and look for "the standards-based classroom," where standards for daily lessons and student objectives are prominently posted. The best advice for all teachers is to know where the curriculum comes from, how the curriculum is guided by standards, and to follow the district and school curriculum guidelines.

Over the past twenty years, many teachers have learned to plan with essential questions (EQs). An essential question is another way to state learning objectives for students. Examples follow:

Objective: The student will be able to add three-digit numbers.
Essential question: How do I add three-digit numbers?
Objective: The student will recognize three genres of literature and be able to list a characteristic of each.
Essential question: What are three genres of literature, and what is a characteristic of each?

Essential questions were introduced in student-friendly terms, and students were supposed to be able to answer the question at the end of a lesson or unit. Many classrooms still have the EQs posted for daily lessons and weekly reviews. It is another way to look at objectives for student learning, striving to make learning explicit.

Gone are the days when teachers went into their classrooms and taught their favorite books, spending much more time on subjects that they personally enjoyed. I worked with an education student who said that she was going to teach *To Kill a Mockingbird* no matter which grade she taught—sixth through twelfth. When I told her about the control that teachers had and didn't have over what was taught, she seemed surprised. "What if every teacher just taught what he or she liked?" I asked. "What if every school just set its own curriculum and students in New York received a very different education than those in Mississippi? Should students in ninth grade in one high school learn very different things than those in the high school 18 miles away?" These questions led the student to see the need for standards as guidelines at the national level, state level, and all the way to the classroom level.

No matter the vocabulary of objectives, essential questions, or learning targets, a well-planned lesson is a must for teaching today's students. Teachers can't waste time because there is so much to teach. We need every teachable moment!

Unit Planning

When I was teaching high school Spanish, unit planning was easy. I had textbooks divided into units, and at the end of each unit, I gave a test. Technically speaking, unit planning should be a little more involved than that. Is unit planning just lesson planning on a bigger scale? Carjuzaa and Kellough (2017) defined a unit as "a major subdivision of a course comprising planned instruction about some central theme, topic, issue, or problem for a period of several days to several weeks" (pp. 119–20).

Elements of a Unit Plan

1. Standards for the unit and rationale (Why are we learning this?)
2. Students' learning objectives (By the end of the unit, TSW know and be able to . . .)
3. Length of time needed for the unit
4. Materials and technologies needed
5. Methods to be employed for teaching this unit
6. Learning experiences for the students
7. Assessments during and at the end of the unit
8. Collaboration with other teachers of the grade/subject

Because of standardized testing, more and more long-term planning is done in collaboration with other teachers under the guidance of curriculum directors. It has become rare for a teacher to have to write all original unit and lesson plans alone. Curriculum mapping has supplemented or replaced some unit planning.

Curriculum Mapping

Consider what a student is exposed to from kindergarten to the senior year in high school. Will two students who complete their education in the same school district have the same curriculum? Should they? What if a student moves to a nearby district or to a nearby state? Have the CCSS ensured that all students learn the same things?

The truth is that only the student knows what his or her curriculum has truly been in his or her school career. With curriculum mapping, teachers, students, parents, and administrators should have a clearer, more systematic way to look at what is taught. Curriculum mapping is vertical—showing a grade-to-grade progression. It is also horizontal, guiding all the teachers of a grade level or subject area to concentrate their teacher on similar subjects.

Heidi Hayes Jacobs is considered a leader in the field of curriculum mapping. Her brief summary of mapping follows:

> Using the procedures in this model, groups of teachers examine maps for discrete and specific purposes, with the goal of improving what they teach and how they teach it. Because the maps are electronic and Web based, all teachers have immediate access to them throughout their school, their state, and the globe. Curriculum mapping is a 21st century means for generating ideas as well as reviewing current curricular practice. (Jacobs, 2010, p. 19)

Some teachers are simply given a curriculum map and told to follow it. This used to be called a "scope and sequence" chart because it listed the scope of what was to be taught and a timeline for teaching. True curriculum mapping is much more because teachers themselves make the maps of what they really teach. They compare what they are teaching with what others are teaching, looking for gaps and repetitions. Students wouldn't want to read the *Diary of Anne Frank* in eighth and ninth grades, nor should this piece of work necessarily be left out of a curriculum.

With mapping, the big picture becomes more visible, and what is taught becomes more organized. Most importantly, mapping allows teachers to see what is taught before and after their grade as well as what is taught across grade and subject areas. Collaborative planning of this type goes a long way in reducing teacher isolation.

Maps should be available to all stakeholders. When parents see the amount of material to be included in a semester or year, they should have more respect for the teacher's work. Post maps in the hallway, and make them available on a school website. I imagine a perfect world where parents even use the curriculum maps to help their children choose library books based on the topics on the map. Families might plan a vacation to see some historic sites being studied by their student.

FAQs and More Suggestions about Planning

1. I always have trouble with timing. How do I know how long something will take? Suggestion: This comes with experience. However, it is always good to keep some "sponge" activities to soak up time when needed. If you run out of time, be sure to plan to cover the material the next day. It is better that students understand three concepts well than being confused by six.
2. When I got my first job, the staff developers in our district taught a daylong seminar on lesson planning. The vocabulary was quite different than what we learned in college, but the results were the same—planning to keep students on task every minute and assessing every step of the way. Why are there such differences from college to real world and from school to school? Suggestion: Just as there is no national curriculum, there is no single way to plan lessons and assessments. When new hires are required to attend training on something they already do well, the best thing to do is to learn one new thing from the training session.
3. I have heard that teachers work over 50 hours a week and that much of that time is on planning. Is there a simpler way to plan? Suggestion: Yes. Each time you teach a lesson, write some comments on the plan about timing and what needs to be changed. Many teachers now plan by writing on their computer so that their plans can be updated quickly. Build a lot of PowerPoints and other lessons on topics that can be reused.
4. Our college professors always said not to rely on the textbook but to be creative. I now teach five 50-minute classes a day, and it's a challenge to make original materials as I plan lessons. Suggestion: Find the very best textbook, supplemental materials, and online resources, and use them. You do not have time to reinvent the wheel every day in your classroom. As an author, I can attest that writing a book is a long, challenging process and you simply cannot be expected to teach and write the book at the same time. That's crazy. Use the best curricular materials you can find. You will add to them anyway but not necessarily all the time or early in your career.
5. How much should I share with other teachers? I feel that the teacher next door is not putting in much time with planning and frequently just asks for my plans and activities. Is this fair? I do want her students to be learning too, and I fear that without my help, they might not. Suggestion: This is a tough question. Can you discuss this with a lead

teacher or department chair? In so many schools, planning is done in grade or subject area groups, and this may be a solution to your issue. The administrator who evaluates the teacher next door will hopefully catch on to this teacher and her or his lack of preparation.

KEYS FOR SUCCESS

1. Successful teachers know that there is a big picture of curriculum—teaching students for the needs of the society and the needs of the individual.
2. Successful teachers know what should be taught and follow standards for teaching.
3. Successful teachers plan lessons with beginnings, middles, and endings. Their lessons have goals and student learning objectives.
4. Successful teachers start with the end in mind, knowing what their students should know and be able to do at the end of lessons, units, and courses.
5. Successful teachers collaborate with regard to what is taught and when it is taught, using curriculum mapping.

Chapter Five

Use Effective Methods and Strategies

Successful teachers select the right method and strategies for every lesson.

This chapter is all about the fun part of teaching—using different methods and strategies for actually teaching! Think about the best learning experiences that you had as a student. How did the teacher make those experiences happen? Were you ever spellbound by a teacher's story? Did a teacher show a picture or a video or bring in an object that captured your attention and made you think? Did you enjoy discussions? Games? Group work? Independent work? Did you get bored doing the same things over and over? Did you ever have a teacher whose main teaching method was handing out worksheets?

Once you know what to teach, then you can decide how to teach. Four questions may guide your choice of teaching methods and strategies:

1. How much of this material do the students already know?
2. How can I teach this material?
3. How can the students learn this material?
4. How will I know that the students learned this material?

ASSESS PRIOR INTEREST AND KNOWLEDGE (APIK)

Our students are not blank slates. Some five-year-olds come to school knowing how to read. Sixth-grade students should know quite a bit of math, but as a seventh-grade teacher, you need to find out how much of that math they remember and can use. Imagine how much a fifteen-year-old may know about the world. If a student spent the summer traveling in Europe or doing volunteer work in Guatemala, your lesson on geography may seem flat to him or her.

How do you find out what students know and how much they know about a curricular topic? Ask them—and ask them in different ways. Some of the ways to assess prior interest and knowledge (APIK) include:

1. Before a unit, have an open-ended discussion about topics that are in that unit. Ask the students what they know about the topics. Some students may volunteer wrong information, and others may say nothing. The downside of open-class discussions is that some students may feel "stupid" because they have nothing to contribute about the topic. Teachers should never make students feel "dumb" about lack of knowledge. This type of APIK activity must be carefully structured by the teacher.
2. Having students write answers to questions about the upcoming topics gives confidentiality to the process of assessing prior knowledge. Tell students you are asking for their input before you plan the lessons of the unit. Don't ask too many questions that start with "What do you know about?" Better questions are specific. Give students some sample math problems or ask them specific questions about social studies or science to find out what they know.
3. Do online assessments. Applications like Kahoot allow students to use their cell phones to answer questions with anonymity and then see the immediate answers on the screen. It makes assessing prior interest and knowledge quick and engaging.
4. Interest inventories about curriculum can be very helpful. For example, before a geography lesson about the countries of South America, ask students to list a country they would like to travel to and why they would choose that country. Provide some information in the inventory. For example, would you rather go skiing in Argentina or hiking in a rain forest in Brazil. Why?
5. Pretests are very helpful in ascertaining what students already know. Pretests have become common because teachers must document their effect on student learning. A pretest is given to students so the teacher can look at the scores for preliminary data and then organize the specifics of the lessons. When the exact same test is given as the final assessment, a teacher has data about each student's learning. A pretest can be as short as ten vocabulary words or as long as a chapter test. Pretests must be administered carefully, and students must know that they are not being graded on what they know at that point. Pretests are becoming more and more common at the beginning of the year in elementary, middle, and high schools. We certainly hope our students do better on the end-of-year assessments after the teaching takes place.

A Practical Example

A sixth-grade teacher taught the first chapter in the math book and gave the accompanying test. Sixty percent of her students failed completely, and most of the others had very weak scores. She thought the reason for the abysmal scores was that students didn't know the major concepts of fifth-grade math, which she hadn't reviewed. Her supervisor reminded her that a sixth-grade math test actually tests the math learned in first, second, third, fourth, and fifth grades. Some pretesting and extensive reviewing would have probably started the year off better.

Once we know what students know, then we can teach them—and we should definitely be teaching them with a variety of methods.

METHOD 1: LECTURE AND PRESENTATION

We generally think of college professors as the teachers who give lectures. But teachers at every grade level talk, and talking is lecturing. When a kindergarten teacher explains how red and white make pink, that's a lecture. When a third-grade teacher presents material on the ways products are transported, that's a lecture. A lecture is a presentation, and there are many ways to improve lectures.

Lectures are a form of direct teaching, and direct teaching received a bad reputation for a while in education. However, direct teaching yields results.

> Direct instruction is a straightforward form of teaching. It helps teachers tackle well-defined content using systemic and chronological instruction based on scripted lessons. Direct instruction often features fast-paced and efficient teacher-student interactions. (Stronge & Xu, 2016)

The advantage of lectures and presentations is that you can convey a lot of material to many students quickly. You can control material and often control classroom management better. To be fair, the downside of lecturing is that students do not necessarily learn by hearing. You can make lectures and presentations work better by modifying them just a bit.

To make any lecture more effective, add visuals on the screen. Show pictures to young children while you talk. Add Internet sites with videos of what you are talking about, and students are more apt to remember material with visual cues. Tell students why there is new material in your lecture/presentation. Write an objective on the board—what they will know or be able to do by the end of the talk. Give students guided notes, and have them follow the lecture by filling in blanks in their notes. This gives them something to listen for while you speak.

Teachers talk too much! We talk too fast, and sometimes, we don't even speak clearly or loudly enough for all students to understand. Good teaching involves good speech communication. Make your voice and your pace appropriate for the age level of your students. Most importantly, limit your time on the stage.

It is important to talk/lecture for a few minutes and then stop to ask students to do something. With elementary students, the teacher must stop frequently and get students involved with questions. With older students, including high school, talking for about eight minutes is the limit. Other guidelines for getting students involved might be:

1. Tell students that you will speak for five minutes and then they will pick up their pencils or open their laptops and write the three most important things you said. After they write, you should then share what you intended the three important things to be. It's more than a guessing game; it's a way to get students to sort and prioritize what they are hearing.
2. After part of a lesson, ask one question. Make sure it's also on the screen, and have students talk for 60 seconds to answer the question. At the end of the minute, ask students to share answers. Called "think, pair, share" by many teachers, this strategy breaks up a lecture and gets students thinking and working.
3. Another way to get students working with material from the lecture is "think, write, pair, share." Ask the question or pose a math problem to be solved, and let students think about it, write an answer, pair up, and then share answers. The quality of answers improves with this strategy, and the lecture or delivery of new material is broken up with short bouts of student engagement.

To summarize, all teachers talk, lecture, and present new material. We are supposed to do this because we are the subject-matter experts. Lecturing alone won't get students to learn, but it is a starting place. When visuals are added to lectures, learning improves. When students engage with the material by writing, problem solving, or explaining to each other, their retention of material improves.

METHOD 2: CONCEPT ATTAINMENT

A concept is an idea, a thought, a theory, an abstraction, or a view. Cruikshank, Bainer, and Metcalf (1995) wrote, "The term concept is used to refer to a group of ideas or objects that are alike and thus share a common name or label." They believed that "a major function of formal education is to teach concepts" (p. 169). In elementary school, teachers teach the most basic of concepts—season, weather, color, family, and so on. As students progress through school, there are myriads of concepts—equality, light, integers, and genre.

The teaching of concepts is tied closely to lectures and presentations because a common way to explain concepts is to give a definition and examples. When teaching about the United States, a teacher defines the concepts of region, state, county, and city. Examples of each concept are presented so that students understand the differences. Students learn that they live in the Midwest, in Illinois, in Morgan County, and in the city of Jacksonville.

Giving a definition with examples is a clear, direct way to teach. The use of nonexamples is also important. Belgium is not a state of the United States. Chicago is not a county in Illinois. Georgia is a state, but not in the Midwest. Nonexamples help students learn to differentiate and sort material.

Concept attainment can also be taught inductively in the style of discovery learning. With this strategy, the teacher begins with applications and leads students to find rules, make comparisons, and create definitions. I used an inductive approach when I taught the concept of past tense in my Spanish classes. Once students knew present-tense verbs, I introduced a dialogue with past-tense verbs. They quickly saw verbs that they sort of recognized but with different endings. "What are the endings you see?" I would ask. As they searched for endings, they were learning the past tense. I summarized the lesson with a graph of verbs in past tense and gave them more verbs to conjugate as a check for understanding.

Review of Teaching with Concept Attainment—Four Easy Steps

A concept is a group of ideas or objects.
  Deduction/expository teaching of a concept:

1. Define the concept clearly. Include attributes of the concept.
2. Provide examples of the concept.
3. Provide nonexamples to help students see the difference.
4. Check for understanding. Provide more examples and nonexamples for students to sort.

Inductive/discovery teaching of a concept:

1. Begin the lesson with something new. Let students "discover" the comparisons among a group of items.
2. As students make comparisons, have them sort examples and nonexamples.
3. Have students make a definition of the concept.

4. Students test their definition, as a hypothesis, as an assessment of their learning. (based in part on Cruikshank, Bainer, & Metcalf, 1995)

Many beginning teachers ask, "Which should I do—direct or discovery when I need to teach a concept?" This is where teaching becomes really fun because the answer is, "It all depends." It depends on the age of the student (remember your ed psych training), the material to be taught, the time given for teaching, and what you know about your teaching style and students' learning styles.

METHOD 3: DEMONSTRATIONS AND MODELING

A demonstration is an extension of a lecture or presentation because it makes learning come alive. A demonstration models concepts that you are teaching. Silver, Strong, and Perini (2007) described modeling as doing: "The skill is modeled by the teacher, who thinks aloud while performing the skill" (p. 35). To create effective modeling in teaching, they wrote:

> A Direct Instruction lesson begins with a good modeling session, which lays out every step in the skill and demonstrates how each step is performed. A good modeling session explains to students what outcomes they are working toward and what is expected of them as they develop the skill. Finally, good modeling means teaching both the steps in performing the skill and thinking aloud to expose the covert thinking that occurs during each step. (p. 38)

Art teachers are great at demonstrations and modeling. Science teachers use demonstrations in every lab. Language arts teachers model writing paragraphs. Although the teacher can do many demonstrations, technology provides us with great demonstrations online. Guest speakers make great models and demonstrators.

After the teacher demonstrates, the students can then practice and become engaged. I once observed a second-grade science lesson where the teacher demonstrated how two cups measured the same as a pint by pouring two cups into a pint jar. Next, she showed how many pints were in a quart and how many quarts were in a gallon. Students were truly engaged when they got to go to stations around the room and measure water in cups, pints, quarts, and gallons. Yes, it got a little messy, but what a good hands-on lesson. Successful teachers are not afraid of a little mess.

METHOD 4: TEACHING WITH QUESTIONS

What makes questioning a good way to teach? Questions make students think, and thinking is the key to learning. The very worst question to ask is,

"Who knows the answer?" The true response to this question is "Suzy knows!" Successful teachers don't ask this question; rather, they ask higher-order questions that promote thinking.

There are many kinds of questions that successful teachers have in their repertoire of teaching. They include:

1. Questions to ascertain prior interest and knowledge (already discussed at the beginning of the chapter).
2. Questions to determine basic comprehension of material read/presented. Also called convergent questions, these questions are narrow and have a single correct answer. They are considered lower-level questions but are important for verifying that students have basic understandings. Hint: "When using questions of this type, try to come back with follow-up questions when possible so the student answering can demonstrate thinking beyond rote memory" (Callahan, Clark, & Kellough, 2002, p. 265). Example: Who was the main character in the story? Follow up with "What made this character the center of the story?"
3. Divergent questions are open ended and lead students to think broadly and reflectively. They are higher-order questions that require analysis, synthesis, or evaluation (Callahan et al., 2002). Examples: "Why would an author write about the theme that she chose for this novel?" "What big topic/theme would you want to write about to make a political statement?"
4. Evaluative questions require students to think and decide. They may involve value judgments or taking a stand. These questions may cause heated debates in classrooms but are important in teaching students how to think through tough decisions. Examples: "Was the main character right or wrong in giving her child up for adoption?" "What would you do in her circumstance?"

    Another type of question is the focus question, which gets students to pay attention to a specific idea or topic. A probing question works well to get students to dig more deeply into material. Cueing is an important part of questioning because it helps students think through their answers and prompts memory. When students can't answer questions, cues aid their thinking. Sometimes, the cue is another question, a hint, or just the first letter of the answer. Example: "Who was the theorist behind the Zone of Proximal Development?" (No answers from the class.) Cue: "His name starts with a V." "Vygotsky," students chime.

METHOD 5: DISCUSSIONS

Good questions lead to good discussions. A set of well-prepared questions can make a discussion that lasts for an entire lesson and leads students to meet the learning objectives. Discussions are excellent for:

1. Previewing material
2. Finding out what students already know
3. Developing deeper understanding of material
4. Reviewing material

> A thoughtful and productive classroom discussion is like a colorful, tightly woven tapestry, as its many threads intertwine in purposeful ways and result in discernable patterns. Like a fine tapestry, a productive discussion does not just happen; it results from planning and skilled craftsmanship. In the case of discussion, it is a teacher's and students' skills in quality questioning that underpin the successful outcome. (Walsh & Sattes, 2015)

Successful teachers know that good discussions don't just happen. They take planning and occur when students have been taught how to discuss. "In teacher-guided discussions, teachers strategically engage and instruct students in classroom conversation while deepening their understanding of content" (Walsh & Sattes, 2015, p. 57). Some strategies and hints for planning discussion include:

1. Go over the guidelines for a discussion before the first one and review the guidelines quickly before each one. Have the guidelines written on a poster or the screen.
2. The guidelines should include classroom management issues—how to take turns, how to address each other, and civility in a discussion.
3. The teacher must have a goal for the discussion and student learning objectives. Don't keep these a secret. Write them on the board or screen, and make them explicit before the discussion and at the end.
4. Knowing that questions drive a discussion, write the questions out well in advance. It can be very helpful to share the questions with students before the discussion begins so that they have time to prepare their answers and their own questions.
5. For accountability, collect students' prepared questions. Inform them that these questions do count as a grade.
6. Monitor time. If the teacher knows in advance that one or two students will monopolize a discussion, then a timing system must be used.
7. Successful teachers know that they must teach students how to listen and how to respond to each other no matter the age of the students.

Educational discussions are not the same as TV debates where people scream at each other.

Many teachers have neglected the use of discussions out of fear of losing control of their class or because of value-laden issues. However, a well-planned discussion with guidelines is a teaching method that promotes civil discussion by the students later in life. What steps make up a good discussion?

Walsh and Sattes (2015) list five stages for the discussion process: preparing, opening, sustaining, closing, and reflecting (p. 63). When teaching my own student teachers about discussion, I have the following steps:

1. Write a lesson plan for the discussion. Start with your goal(s) and the students' objectives. Write out questions.
2. Focus the students on the objectives of the discussion and the guiding rules for discussion.
3. Keep the momentum going! Let students talk, but remember that they need interventions and guidance. Use your questions and the students' questions.
4. A good discussion has a closing where the teacher assesses what students learned and what points need to be reviewed explicitly. (Students can share wrong information in a discussion, and those false statements need to be addressed.)
5. Have some follow-up student work for accountability/assessment.

METHOD 6: GROUP WORK

Successful teachers know that trends, and even fads, come and go in education. Group work and cooperative learning are not fads but valid ways of getting students to learn how to work with others. However, students should not be grouped all the time, nor should they be placed in the same groups for long amounts of time—like an entire semester. Additionally, even in group work, grading should be done for the completion of individual work within a group.

What are the general guidelines for making group work succeed?

1. Students have to have a clear set of objectives to complete. There must be a reason for the group to be formed and to work.
2. Time frames must be stated and followed.
3. Groups have to be monitored.
4. The group is held accountable for their work. The work may be a product, an answer, a presentation, or other proof of work.

5. Individuals should be graded on their work, to be fair to all.
6. When group work has been completed, a teacher should be explicit about what was learned about content and about the process of the work. It is always good to relate the process to the real world.

Cooperative learning can be considered a subset of grouping. Not all grouping activities are true cooperative learning and don't need to be. Marzano, Pickering, and Pollock (2001) recommend the use of cooperative learning in the Johnson and Johnson style (p. 85). Their recommendations include careful consideration of how groups are formed, keeping groups small, and not overusing this method. Cooperative learning is known for having specific jobs for each student, including group manager, timekeeper, recorder, and presenter of information. Giving students specific duties will help with any group work.

What are some good uses of group work? Group work is productive for brainstorming, reviewing, role-playing, and problem solving.

1. At the beginning of a new unit or theme, groups of three can make a list of everything they know, or think they know, about the topic. When time is up, groups share. (Remember that some groups will share incorrect information. The teacher needs to be ready to address misinformation in a diplomatic way.)
2. Groups can make a KWL chart together about a new topic. The K is knowledge, or what they know; the W is what they want to learn about the topic. At the end of the lesson or unit, the groups get back together to complete their charts with what they learned (the L).
3. Pairs or small groups can work together on big-issue questions or problems to solve. The big question is on the screen, or the math or science problem, and groups work together on the problem. They may present their solution in front of the class or on the Smart Board at the end of a monitored amount of time.
4. Groups can be given role-plays to plan and perform. After reading a story or play, the small groups can act out a short scene or read a special part of the assigned work with some acting.
5. Role-plays include acting out how to shop in a market, how to eat in a foreign restaurant, or how to run for governor or president. Students enjoy creativity and learn from these activities.
6. Group work is good for reviewing. A group can write questions for an upcoming test, and the teacher may use one question from each group. Ask students "If you were writing this test, what would you put on the test?"

METHOD 7: TEACHING WITH PROJECTS

Everyone can probably remember his or her science project. Did you *really* do the project yourself, or did you have significant help from a family member? Successful teachers use projects wisely, ensuring that there are objectives for the projects and that every student can achieve success.

A project is assigned when students need time to explore a particular topic or when they can do a bit of research to deepen their understanding. Individual students can complete a project, or projects can be completed by groups. Here are the issues a teacher must decide before using projects to extend student learning.

1. Why am I choosing the project? What is the student objective for the project? Answer the question "By the end of the project, the student will know or be able to . . ."
2. How much time will the project take? Will all the time be given in class?
3. What is the end result of the project—a paper, a presentation, or a video?
4. What materials do students need, and how are the materials provided?
5. Will students work in groups, and if so, why?
6. How will the project be assessed?

There are other issues when using projects in the classroom. Does the school culture (community, economic levels of families) allow for the expectation that students can provide their own materials? If not, all materials must be provided by the school and work completed during school time.

What is the expectation of parental/family help with projects? If a student's father is a professor of mathematics and students are making math projects, how does a teacher limit the parent from just doing the project, or should the teacher be delighted that the parent can extend the learning of the student? The teacher should create clear criteria so that students and families have guidelines for projects.

All of the recommendations for successful group work also apply to project work. These include clear objectives to be met, timelines for the projects, and student accountability. It is always a good idea to set due dates for each step of the project and not just allow students to work or not work with a final project due on a certain day.

METHOD 8: LAB WORK

One of my very favorite science classes in middle school was one where we planted trees. Going outside and planting trees and knowing that, in three years, we could return and actually have a tree for our own yard was the greatest lab ever. My tree is still growing at my mother's house and is probably over 40 feet tall now. My teacher was very successful about teaching us to appreciate trees, and he was one of my favorite teachers.

Lab work is important for hands-on learning. Science teachers have long known the need for students to apply the theory from a textbook in the lab. Doing one's own experiments reinforces learning in a way that has a lasting effect. (I will always respect trees.)

Science labs have changed considerably down through the years. The expenses of maintaining labs has skyrocketed. Working with dead animals in labs has become a thing of the past for multiple reasons. However, viewing labs through online programs provides wonderful and free virtual-reality labs.

Besides science, how can teachers incorporate a lab-type learning experience into their classrooms? Learning centers are a type of lab. Students rotate through the centers (labs) to complete different types of activities. There may be readings, things to write, websites to search, or a hands-on project at each station. Writing labs are indeed labs, as are art projects.

Foreign language labs are a great example of how to make subject content come alive. With today's technology, students can tour the Louvre Museum in Paris or hike on Machu Picchu through virtual reality. They can mimic a native speaker with high-tech language apps and sing along with the most hip of international singers. Yes, labs can work for subjects other than just science.

METHOD 9: TEACHING WITH GAMES

Did you like games when you were a student? Did you learn from games? What are the pros and cons of using games in the classroom? How do successful teachers use games to enhance student learning?

First of all, not all students like games because they feel that they will never win. Some students don't like the competition and don't want their knowledge, or lack of knowledge, to be put on public display. On the other hand, some students love games and will do extra preparation to be ready for a review game. In other words, a game might motivate some serious study.

What are some guidelines for using games as a method of teaching?

1. The game should fit a lesson objective. For example, "By the end of the game, the students will have reviewed twenty-five vocabulary words that will be on the next chapter test."
2. Classroom management should already be well established before the teacher uses a game.
3. Specific procedures and rules should be taught each time a game is used. These procedures and rules should also be posted for students to see.
4. Individual competition should not be the focus of the game. The old-time spelling bee is not a good game because it pits individuals against each other. The weakest students, who need the most review, are the ones who have to sit out of the game first, and then they tend to pay no attention.
5. The use of high-tech gaming can be useful in today's classrooms (more about this in chapter 6).
6. Cooperation needs to be taught to students in a game.
7. A game shouldn't just be a time filler. Having students earn a game as a positive for good behavior makes the game serve two purposes—a reward and a teaching method.
8. Strive not to hand out prizes or candy to winning teams. Winning should be its own reward.
9. Remember developmental readiness and school culture when considering a game as a teaching method. A game may not be a good choice for very young children or for every classroom culture.

KEYS FOR SUCCESS

1. Successful teachers are strategic in choosing which methods work for their students.
2. Successful teachers vary the methods they use in teaching.
3. Successful teachers are sometimes very direct, and other times they elicit student learning through discovery learning and more indirect methods.
4. Successful teachers use research-based methods to improve student learning.
5. Successful teachers incorporate hands-on methods as much as possible.
6. Successful teachers know to consider who the students are, what the content is, and the culture of the school when considering how to teach.
7. Successful teachers continue to look for successful teaching methods.

Chapter Six

Use Technology

Successful teachers know when and how to incorporate technology.

In the summer of 2017, I taught a graduate class to a group of principals in China. Months before I arrived in China to teach the class, I began gathering my materials. All of the materials I used to teach were original and written by me. The reading assignments were articles and a chapter I had published; there were PowerPoints for each class session. Three weeks before the class was to start, I uploaded all the material into Moodle, on a series of pages designed specifically for my class by the system administrator at the college.

This is where the story gets interesting. The college had translators to translate the readings into Mandarin and then post those versions of the material. The 14 students in the class could access the material before I even arrived in China. When I did arrive and started teaching, the room was arranged so that each student had his or her laptop out on a desk. Students listened to my teaching, through a translator, and pulled up my PowerPoints as I spoke. They saw the English and wrote notes beside the PPT slides in Chinese. For the materials that were already translated, they still took notes next to the translation on their laptops.

They turned in their assignments in Moodle. I graded each assignment and posted the grade, with extensive comments, on the same Moodle page. As soon as my grading was done, they received their feedback instantly. These students studied a lot, almost constantly, so the comments I wrote one night were read by the students before class the next day. The last assignment for the class was not due until I was home in the United States, and I graded those final assignments on my computer in my home office.

This was a good use of technology to span time and space for classroom teaching. The materials could be provided without the need for students to purchase a book. The instant feedback added greatly to the discussions in class the next day.

Now, let's look at other scenarios. In one state, all third-graders must take their standardized writing test on their laptop computers. Fortunately, in most schools, there are enough laptops that each student can complete exercises on a laptop throughout the year before the high-stakes test. However, is this a test of writing or a test of keyboarding? Are third-grade students developmentally ready to type on a keyboard for a test? Do they even have the finger dexterity to do so?

In a seventh-grade math classroom, all students have a laptop. For 60 minutes of the 90 minutes they are in math class, they are on their laptops, doing different exercises. For 30 minutes of the time, they receive instruction from the teacher. Is this a good division of their time? Is it a good use of the teacher's time?

In a ninth-grade English class, the students pull out their laptops for a pretest on the Kahoot application. The pretest shows that students really don't understand the concept of active voice versus passive voice. They practice with a handout/worksheet, because they have no textbooks, and take the same Kahoot application as a posttest at the end of class. The scores are only marginally better, and for many of the examples, almost half the class can't determine whether a given sentence is active or passive voice. However, the teacher does know instantly that more time must be devoted to the topic.

In a high school Spanish class, the teacher presents a visual lesson on the Smart Board about the royal family of Spain. The lesson centers on learning the Spanish words for extended family members as well as learning some cultural stories about Spain. Students are then asked to write on their laptops about their own family members. They are asked whether they would like to be a queen or king, like the royalty of Spain? How would they describe themselves, as a son, daughter, sister, brother, or even as a king or queen? The teacher logs on to her laptop and can view what each individual student is writing. The lesson has combined culture, grammar, and vocabulary very well, with current pictures of the Spanish royals.

Many questions arise from each of these classroom stories where technology is used. Is the individual technology worth the cost of it? When a district invests in what is called one-to-one technology, where each student has a laptop for school use, is the cost more than keeping current textbooks in the classroom? Who makes these technology decisions? Should it be a director of curriculum or a technology expert, or should teachers and administrators be involved? There is no one right answer, but let's look at what teachers can do with technology and how it might be incorporated into classrooms.

Specifically, we can look at:

1. Simple uses of technology
2. Computers for practice, reinforcement of learning, and assessment
3. Guidelines and ideas
4. Gaming in the classroom
5. What the future might hold

SIMPLE USES OF TECHNOLOGY

When I first attended a distance-learning workshop, the presenter said, "Distance learning with technology makes a good teacher look better and makes a bad teacher look worse." Interesting! Why might this be true? Adding technology to teaching should not be something teachers do to prove that they are using technology. Just as the elementary teachers have learned that "cute has to count," so too do all teachers need to learn that technology may or may not be what is needed to enhance their teaching and students' learning.

First and foremost, technology is a great aid for clerical duties. Use technology to simplify your grading system with a spreadsheet. Most schools have purchased a software package for attendance and grading, and all teachers use the system. Some current ones include MasteryConnect, Khan Academy, and Gooru, and these sites offer tremendous independent learning opportunities.

Communication with colleagues, administrators, and families is greatly enhanced with technology. My friend receives text messages with pictures of her son in his preschool throughout the day. This really made her feel less concerned about his welfare those first few weeks of school.

Teacher blogs and classroom websites have become more of the norm than the exception. The biggest caution is that each teacher must adhere to the district guidelines about postings. Additionally, no photos of students can be posted without the express written consent of parents. So what could a teacher put on the site or in the blog?

1. The class calendar of events
2. Names of books, videos, and other class materials and where families can access them
3. The school's procedures for snow days or early dismissal days
4. The class's curriculum map of content and assessments
5. Vocabulary lists and how to help the student learn the words
6. Study guides for units
7. Guidelines for projects

Internet sites make so many classes come alive with visuals. The French teacher can take students on a virtual tour of the Louvre, and the German teacher can locate a current newspaper in German for students to read. The science teacher can show cells dividing, and the history teacher can use myriads of sites for authentic readings that have been posted. Using technology for visuals is a great use of it, and only one computer and projection system are needed.

In my own classroom, I have found that the document camera is a wonderful piece of technology. I create notes for my lectures/presentations in 24-size fonts. Then, I print the notes and share them on the document camera. Students like seeing the questions from readings on the screen as they work to answer them. Yes, I do PowerPoints too, but students at the college level are already burned out on PPTs, and rate my visuals on the screen with the document camera very highly. A colleague of mine actually places the textbook on her document camera from time to time to show students where to find the information she is discussing.

Students can use technology to present their book reports and research papers. They need to be incorporating technology into their presentations because it will be expected in college and the world of work. Making their own videos tends to engage students.

COMPUTERS FOR PRACTICE, REINFORCEMENT, AND ASSESSMENT

Drill and practice (called drill and kill by some) have been downplayed by the educational community over the past fifteen years, yet deep learning requires drills, practice, and reinforcement of material. This is where technology can be of fantastic value. Whether it's practicing division problems or learning vocabulary, computerized programs provide multiple opportunities for students to practice and receive instant feedback.

When searching for valuable programs for students, look for ones that provide instruction, vary the questions, repeat some of them, and make the questions more difficult as students progress through material. Make sure that you can have access to students' scores from the program. Students will enjoy programs that give them stars or badges for moving up the ladder of accomplishment.

Much has been written about meeting individual student's needs, independent learning, and personalized learning. Technology is touted as a solution for meeting the needs of individual students. Arnett (2017) wrote:

> Software can help teachers gather student learning data, analyze that data to pinpoint the daily strengths and struggles of each student, and then deploy various online, teacher-led, independent, and peer-to-peer learning experiences to target students' idiosyncratic learning needs. (para. 7)

Yes, having students take a quiz on Kahoot does give the teacher data on what the students know as class starts. Having them retake the same quiz or a similar one at the end of the lesson provides information about what was learned and whether the objectives were met. Between the pre- and posttests, there should be instruction targeted to the errors noted in the pretest. The value of having instant feedback cannot be overlooked. Imagine the difference between the use of Kahoot in one 50-minute high school English class for assessment of learning compared to a paper-and-pencil test that would be graded and returned to students two days later.

Another practical way to use technology is for large classes that do a lot of problem solving in class. I saw this demonstrated in a college physics class with about fifty students. The professor taught how to solve a specific problem and then projected a similar problem on the screen. The professor had four possible answers on the screen. Students worked the problem and then logged in to the system with their answers using clickers. The professor could quickly see how many students were arriving at the right answer and could diagnose misconceptions leading to the incorrect answers.

If your school doesn't have clickers, polleverywhere.com has the same capabilities, and students use their personal cell phones to log in to the system. Virtually all high school students have cell phones. If they don't, pair students together to share phones. Apps exist for this type of use on tablets as well.

Standardized testing of students is not going away. These tests are administered via computers, so students must have practice throughout the year with applications similar to the standardized tests. A big part of success on standardized tests may quickly become the student's ability to use the technology of the test. Third-graders do need to know how to write quickly and accurately on a laptop to pass their standardized writing test. Typing used to be in the high school curriculum but has been replaced with keyboarding, which is in many elementary school programs. We have to be careful to prepare students in how to use technology, and sometimes, that means backing up and teaching some basics first. Learning how to type/use the keyboard with something like Typing Tutor (www.typingtutor-online.com/en/aspx/Start.aspx) may be a good starting point.

GUIDELINES AND IDEAS

The Flipped Classroom

The flipped classroom is an idea that has been implemented in elementary, middle, and high schools. In its simplest form, flipping the classroom involves having students watch the teacher present new information at home in lieu of homework and then come to class prepared to ask questions about the material and to work related problems in class. This is different than the teacher presenting the material in class and then having students work problems at home as homework. Advantages include more time for the teacher to individualize instruction, instant feedback to the students as they work, and more opportunities for students to collaborate in class.

The flipped classroom is not just for math and science where problem solving is a large component of the learning process. Students in history and language arts can view or listen to their teachers' lectures about the topic and then read material and come to class ready to discuss material. They can view the author of their assigned reading discuss his or her work or view a documentary about the historical era they are studying.

At Minnesota's Byron High School, teachers experienced tremendous success with the flipped classroom (Fulton, 2012). Fulton wrote:

> With class time freed up from lectures, teachers are developing open-ended, cross-curricular projects that actively engage students and bring real-life relevance to their math skills. And, because of eighth grade teacher Jeremy Baumbach's involvement in the math curriculum redesign, some middle school students are already experiencing flipped classes. (p. 17)

Success for the flipped classroom depends on many factors.

1. Students must have access to technology at home because the teacher's lectures and videos are posted online.
2. Students must watch and listen to the material at home or after school somewhere—in a school-supervised setting or at a public library.
3. Teachers must have time to create videos or select online materials for students to listen to, watch, or read. Selection and production of material takes time and equipment.
4. Parents have to be informed and made aware of the value of this type of teaching with technology.
5. In-class work must be monitored strictly, allowing for students to work thoughtfully and diligently.
6. The school administration must be onboard with the flipped classroom because some administrators still want to see teacher-led classrooms when they complete formal evaluations of teachers.
7. Assessment is critical. Teachers who implement flipped classrooms need to become researchers of their own practice to verify whether flipping is indeed serving students.

There are indeed pitfalls and issues with the flipped classroom. Naysayers contend that if they teach in a school whose students never do any homework outside of the classroom, how can they get students to spend the equivalent time watching lectures, presentations, and related documentaries? When high school students work 20 to 40 hours a week or participate in team sports that require most of their after-school time, when would they have any time to prepare for the flipped classroom? Might these students come to class even further behind?

The technology itself is a huge issue with the flipped classroom. The technology has to work, and work well consistently. It has to be provided by the school for issues of equity for all students. What happens when a student loses a school-owned laptop? When does the teacher have time to create meaningful presentations? Who helps the teacher make the technology work?

One teacher said the following in a workshop that I attended:

> We have always expected students to prepare outside of class. They were expected to read a chapter with examples and be ready for class with their questions. In English classes, we expected students to read the novel and come to class to discuss it. In the flipped classroom, we now expect them to watch or listen to something and come prepared for class. However, in the last several years, I can't get my students to do anything outside of class. It's the culture of the school that everything be done during school hours, with no homework. In some classes, the whole book is read aloud in literature classes (ninth grade). How do we change the culture of nothing being done outside of class to having students diligently work one to two hours a night on their schoolwork just because it's on a laptop?

This quote indicates the issues of the flipped classroom quite clearly. The school must make a paradigm shift for this to work. Students and their families would have to see the value of working on school assignments at home.

One of the biggest issues I have seen with the flipped classroom is that teachers think that they have to do the flipping every day of every week of the semester. No! This is not the case. A teacher should consider easing in to the process with one or two days a week of flipping the classroom. Better yet, use the flipped classroom when the curriculum fits this format. Teachers should consider the flipped classroom another method for teaching, not the one and only best single method to be used every day.

More Technology Guidelines

Technology is expensive and has to be maintained and updated. A school district cannot expect its teachers to implement and use technology without sufficient support and training. Some companies are selling laptops to schools at deeply discounted prices, provided that teachers in those schools use the laptops. The companies then sell software to the schools because not everything needed to teach the curriculum is provided for free online. There is often no money left for traditional textbooks or other supplies.

A first-year teacher was hired in a district with laptops for every student. She had no textbook for her Spanish class nor was there an electronic textbook available for the laptops. She searched every day for the appropriate free materials and practice drills for her students. As she said, "It was like I was writing my own textbook, and as a first-year teacher, that was really tough!" In another district, all the math textbooks were thrown away, and teachers were told to read the state's curriculum guide and to create their own textbook from online materials. Again, this is no easy task for teachers.

There is a very old phrase that says, "Don't throw the baby out with the bathwater." When implementing technology, the timeline and introduction must be reasonable. Yes, teachers should make use of available technology, but they should also remember that computers will never replace teachers.

Gaming in the Classroom

My friend's son likes to stay up all night "on the computer." He is a whiz at multiple games and reads anime (Japanese animation) online for hours. How can his attraction to this type of gaming and reading be transferred to academic work? This young man has tremendous concentration skills when it comes to gaming and the twists and turns of complicated anime plots. Now, teachers, how do we make his concentration skills transferable to what he needs to learn in the classroom?

Students want to read when the readings interest them. Stufft, Abrams, and Gerber (2016) found that when young adult literature (YAL) is compared to video game playing and movie watching, richer class discussions ensued. (2016). Their research involved making book groups more relevant by allowing and encouraging students to relate ideas from YAL books to the forms of media they were involved with outside of class—namely video games and movies.

> In this sense, book groups provide a space for students to share gaming experiences and to refer to other media of interest as they interpret a YA text; the book group can act as a springboard for students to continue to learn both within and beyond school. (Stufft et al., 2016, p. 98)

When I had the opportunity to hear the lead author of this article (Stufft) speak, I found myself asking many questions. (My questions revealed that I am clearly not a gamer.)

1. Do video games have plots and characters?
2. How expensive are these games, and how many students are playing them? Do all students have access to video games?

3. How much time are students spending on these games?
4. Can genre be taught better through gaming than through traditional texts?
5. How do teachers "create spaces" in their classrooms for students to hook video games to literary content?
6. Does adding the video-game component to discussions validate students' experiences in their world?

Prior to hearing Stufft speak, it had never crossed my mind that video games had any educational purpose. She convinced me that a video game could be used for critical analysis of a text just as a piece of classical literature might. That's a big leap for many of us. Technology does open up a whole new world for educators, and it's an area worthy of much more exploration.

WHAT MIGHT THE FUTURE HOLD?

Arnett (2017) wrote that "The future of learning technology is not replacing teachers, but amplifying their ability to meet the learning needs of their students" (para. 1). Armstrong (2018) wrote that today's teachers are teaching to the "picture smart" individual and that technology brings visual images into the classroom more quickly than ever before.

> A student who's reading a Victorian novel and runs across the word *brougham* has only to search Google Images (or one of the many other image libraries online) to see the cute little carriages that carried people around in the 19th century. Similarly, a teacher who is teaching a unit in history can usually find a three- to five-minute documentary with historical footage that can grab Picture Smart learners and excite them enough to engage with the material in the classroom textbook. (p. 175)

Of course, technology has already changed how teachers, and students, do research. When a teacher asked students to make an annotated bibliography of books on a certain topic, she didn't expect that some students would simply go to amazon.com, type in the topic, and cut and paste information from the site for their bibliographies. The teacher was appalled when her students did this and felt she should fail them on the assignment. With such a wealth of information available online, teachers do need to set clear criteria and parameters for their assignments.

I was actually impressed that these students were savvy users of online resources, and I thought she should make another assignment where students used amazon.com as the only resource to find books about a topic. Then, the teacher could discuss online resources versus libraries as well as the validity of reviews on Amazon. All kinds of questions can ensue. Who writes the reviews on Amazon? Should we believe every review? Find a book review on Amazon for a book you have read. Do you agree or disagree with the reviewer? Write a review and post it online. The possibilities are endless.

Some other ideas and questions for online research include:

1. Look at a site like Wikipedia. Who posts the research there? How valid are these postings? Find a site with current information, and read to see whether you find any questionable information.
2. Read a magazine article online. Who wrote the article? Did anyone have to review the author's work before it was published online?
3. Do a search online for a specific topic. Did you find any information that had no author? Without an author, how valid/usable is this information to you in writing a paper or making a presentation?
4. How do you cite online material if you are writing a paper or making a presentation? What if there is no date on the material you found?
5. Is material that is online more reliable if it is also published in a paper journal?

Online Classes

Online classes are the current version of old distance-learning programs. In geographically isolated locations (think Australia or even Alaska), students once listened to a teacher via radio and sat at a table in their home with books and papers in front of them. Their papers were turned in for grading via mail services, and tests were either mailed to them or they had to go to a centralized location to "sit" for exams. Now, online classes have changed that format by at least 100 percent.

Students today can be homeschooled with a curriculum not only approved by their state's department of education but also provided free of charge by that department. Teachers can use all or part of the same online curriculum in their classrooms. What are the advantages and issues for online learning for K–12 students?

Advantages:

1. A student in a small school system can take a class online that is not offered in the school. Examples might include upper-division science classes or foreign languages.
2. For some students, focusing on the computer allows them to concentrate because they are the picture-smart, screen-smart generation.
3. Feedback to the student is instant. Programs are geared to have students move on to more difficult material when ready.

4. Learning independently is a skill that students will need long after graduation. Learning how to find information online and learn from it are very important skills.
5. Teachers simply cannot know everything and cannot create original lessons for every content area in the time provided for them to prepare for classes. Using online class materials can save much preparation time.

Issues:

1. There is much debate about the socialization of children who sit in front of screens for much of their learning. Yes, online chat rooms for academic purposes can provide high-level discussion formats, but they may not be the same as being around others.
2. How good are online classes? Do the authors of online courses have the expertise to create powerful learning experiences? Do the instructors of online courses know the material and the developmental readiness of the learners?
3. If the students are taking online courses in the classroom, what is the role of the classroom teacher? Do these teachers become coaches or proctors? Do the teachers need to be online constantly to ensure that the curriculum matches that of their school?
4. Some teachers whose students are using online courses find that the students want them to be available 24/7 for assistance. Again, boundaries have to be drawn.
5. Although many programs are free, not all are. How do teachers evaluate programs for their value?

KEYS FOR SUCCESS

1. Successful teachers use technology to make the day-to-day work of teaching easier.
2. Successful teachers stay current on trends in technology.
3. Successful teachers try new technologies but do not jump on every bandwagon or fad.
4. Successful teachers know that technology can enhance high-quality teaching with visuals, online resources, and pertinent applications.
5. Successful teachers strive to have a say in how technology is implemented schoolwide.
6. Successful teachers stay open minded when new technologies are discussed and offered in their schools.

7. Successful teachers strive to know what technologies their students are already using and to incorporate those into the classroom experience.

Chapter Seven

Assess Student Work

Successful teachers know that assessment is so much more than the dreaded standardized test.

Every spring in America, teachers and students face the much-dreaded standardized testing season. In some states, several weeks are lost because of test preparation, test review, and the testing. Some teachers lament that if they could just teach during all the time given to testing, students would learn more. Although testing is a part of assessment, assessment includes so much more.

Why do we do so much assessment, and just what is assessment? Assessment is a process for finding out information. It's the process for finding out what students are learning or determining how a program is working. We assess to:

1. Assist and improve student learning
2. Identify and/or remediate students' strengths and weaknesses
3. Check on the effectiveness of a program or teaching method or strategy
4. Provide data to families about their child's progress
5. Provide data about school effectiveness
6. Provide data for decision making

A REVIEW OF THE VOCABULARY OF ASSESSMENT

1. Evaluation: making sense of what is found through assessment and making judgments about the assessment

2. Measurement: quantifiable data about specific learning/behaviors/programs
3. Validity: the degree to which a measuring instrument actually measures what it is intended to measure
4. Reliability: the accuracy with which a technique consistently measures what it does measure
5. Authentic assessment: when assessment procedures match instructional objectives
6. Performance assessment: type of student response being assessed
7. Diagnostic assessment (also called preassessment): assessing a student's knowledge before instruction
8. Formative assessment: assessing the student's learning during instruction
9. Summative assessment: the assessment of learning after instruction, generally represented with a grade or pass/fail. (See, for example, Carjuzaa & Kellough, 2017.)

INFORMAL, FORMATIVE ASSESSMENTS

Successful teachers know that they can assess what a student says, what a student does, and what a student writes. These assessments are often ongoing, informal, and formative. Assessment is automatic for a veteran teacher, who pays attention to students' facial expressions, body language, and level of engagement. The first use of informal assessment is to decide how the lesson is being received. Highly successful teachers can change gears in the middle of a lesson if informal assessment indicates a need to do so.

What are some specific informal assessments that are useful?

1. Ask questions throughout a lesson.
2. Ask for more than one response to get more students involved.
3. Have students write and share responses. (Younger children use individual whiteboards and hold up answers to give the teacher quick feedback.)
4. Use technology for quick, anonymous responses (consider clickers or Kahoot).
5. Walk around the room and monitor individual and group work.
6. Observe/be cognizant of the class climate. (Are students engaged or bored?)

ASSESS TO OBJECTIVES

A beginning teacher might teach a chapter in a textbook and then ask, "What should I put on the test?" An experienced, and successful teacher, already knows that tests are written to the predetermined objectives. For an individual lesson, there should be one or more objectives, each stated in the form of "the student will." Throughout the lesson, the teacher strives to determine whether the students are indeed meeting the objective. Hopefully, the students may even be exceeding the objective! Simple examples include:

1. Objective: By the end of the lesson, the student will be able to write an opening sentence for a paragraph.

    Assessment: The student writes an opening sentence and turns it in to the teacher at the end of the lesson.

2. Objective: Given a map, students will be able to identify the state, its capital, and two rivers.

    Assessment: Given a map, students identify the state, its capital, and two rivers.

It is the alignment of objectives to assessments that gives validity to the assessment.

Additionally, students should be assessed in the ways that they were taught the material. In a beginning foreign language class, for example, greetings and good-byes are taught verbally. Students may not see the written word. Students know that *hola* means hello, but it would not be a valid assessment to test the students on the spelling of the word *hola* until after they had seen the spelling, learned about silent *h*, and practiced writing greetings. A better assessment would be a performance one, where students spoke to each other with the appropriate greeting or good-bye.

Everyone immediately thinks of tests and quizzes when assessment is mentioned. Yes, paper-and-pencil testing is a very common assessment. Other ways to assess include:

1. Checklists of a student's accomplishments
2. A log, or anecdotal record, of material learned
3. Rubrics for papers, projects, and presentations
4. Portfolios
5. Observation notes

Checklists provide anecdotal information as well as specific information about what the student knows and is able to do. In the early grades, a checklist might yield information about how many sight words a student knows or how many math problems a student can solve. With older students, a checklist can serve as a benchmark for how much material is covered and guides students to monitor their own work and timeline. Example: a six-step checklist for completion of a paper.

1. Topic chosen
2. Four references found
3. Introduction and first page completed
4. Rough draft
5. Peer editing
6. Final paper turned in

Learning logs, or journals of learning, are somewhat similar. Students keep a log of how many problems completed or how many poems read in a unit. The logs are reviewed by the teacher and feedback provided.

Rubrics have become so common that they are used from kindergarten through graduate school now. A rubric is simply a way to give students specific criteria for an assignment, with specified performance measures. Points are awarded for the performance measures, and the grading of the assignment becomes much more objective. Figure 7.1 is an example of a rubric for an assignment.

Of course, many successful teachers have their students make the rubric, discussing the important points of the assignment. You can start a discussion with the question "What am I looking for in an A paper?" or "What does it take to get a passing grade on this assignment, and what does it take to get the grade you want?" Students may make tougher criteria than you would! A rubric will definitely help you to assess projects, speeches, and other work that is not paper and pencil.

Portfolios are more than just collections of work. A good portfolio helps guide student reflection on their work. For each artifact that students place in a portfolio, they should write why they chose that paper or project to represent their learning. A portfolio can provide evidence of mastering a standard, or it can show growth from the beginning of the year to the end of the year.

Are portfolio assessments difficult to assess? They can be, but by determining the standards in advance and creating an evaluation tool, the grading of a portfolio becomes very doable.

Observation notes are another assessment that helps the teacher learn what students know. The key to good notes is to remember that behaviors are recorded, not opinions! The teacher writes verbatim notes of what a student says or does, without interjecting a judgment. Example:

Scott read 17 sight words; Sept. 6
Not: Scott is behind his peers and seems to lag behind every day (judgment).

8th Grade Book Review Rubric

Criteria	3 Points	2 Points	1 Point
Author's Background	3 Clear Points About Author	2 Clear Points About Author	1 Clear Point About Author
The Book's Theme	3 Clear Points About Theme	2 Clear Points About Theme	1 Clear Point About Theme
Summary of Plot	3 Clear Points About Plot	2 Clear Points About Plot	1 Clear Point About Plot
Reasons to Recommend	3 Reasons to Recommend	2 Reasons to Recommend	1 Reason to Recommend
Grammar/ Spelling	Fewer than 3 Errors	4-5 Errors	6 or More Errors
Length	3 Pages	2 Pages	1 Page

Figure 7.1.

CREATING TESTS

Even with all of the rubrics, checklists, and anecdotal records used in today's schools, testing remains a staple of assessment. Tests are quantifiable ways to measure students' learning. Although some educators may argue that "some students just don't test well," testing is here to stay. What are some best practices in test writing and for the preparation of students for testing?

More and more teachers use prewritten tests that accompany their textbooks. Why? Because these tests mimic the format and content of the end-of-year standardized tests. Prewritten tests save time, and if they are given in an electronic format, they can be graded instantly. If the teacher is using prewritten tests, some guidelines for use are important:

1. Make sure that everything on the test was taught and practiced in the classroom.
2. Check the test and the answer key for mistakes or misinformation.
3. Review the vocabulary on the test. Does it match the vocabulary taught?

4. Read the instructions on the test to verify that students will know what to do on each section.
   5. If the tests are photocopied for use, is there enough space for students to write? Are the copies clear and easy to read?

When Making Your Own Tests

Some teachers consider it their job to write their own tests, and some consider it the only way to ensure that the material tested was the material taught. When making your own tests, consider these guidelines:

   1. Write the test *before* you teach the unit. What? Not the night before? When you look at the objectives for a unit or chapter, that is indeed the time to write the test. Then, teach the material.
   2. Include written instructions on the test for what students are to do. With written instructions, students can't say, "But I didn't know you wanted me to do that."
   3. Create a test with space between the questions to help students do a better job on the test. The test should be double spaced and very clear to read.
   4. Leave large spaces for fill-in-the-blank questions to help students.
   5. Leave large spaces for writing short answers.
   6. Use a variety of test questions. Consider multiple choice, fill in the blank, matching, short answer, essay, and true/false.
   7. Create the key before giving the test. How long did it take you to complete the test? Double that time for your students to write the answers and complete the test. Although there is no way to ensure that this is the amount of time students will need, it is a good starting point for determining time.
   8. When administering a test, separate students as much as possible.
   9. Always proctor tests. This means that you stand and walk around the room, monitoring student work.
   10. Teach students how to take tests—no matter the age of the students. All students need to learn and improve upon their test-taking skills.
   11. If grading a paper-and-pencil test, grade page by page. This means that you grade each student's page one, then each student's page two, and so on until completion. This helps you to remember what you seek in answers, and it helps you *not* to know who each student is. It is hard not to be biased if you look at all of Johnny's test at once and then all of Suzie's test.

Kinds of Test Questions

What were your favorite test questions? Did you like true/false because you had a 50/50 chance of getting the right answer? Was matching helpful because you didn't have to produce an original answer, just mark another word or phrase? How did you feel about multiple guess questions? Did those questions assess what you really learned, or did you just guess, hoping that B was a valid answer?

Now that you are the teacher and deciding what to put on a test, a different set of questions need to be answered.

1. Are my questions easy to devise and is the test user friendly for students to take?
2. Are my questions easy for me to grade? (Maybe doable to grade is a better way to think about this question. Your work grading tests is not necessarily easy but should be doable for your workload.)
3. Do the questions align with the objectives of the material and how the material was taught?
4. Am I trying to assess each individual student's learning or trying to compare student learning and rank my students? In elementary, middle, and high schools, we should be assessing individual's learning. Even colleges and graduate schools are eliminating the rank order value of testing.
5. What does my test reveal to me about my teaching? Should I have spent more time on the topics? Should I have reviewed the material more with students? Am I expecting them to have background knowledge that they don't have?

Writing Test Questions

Perhaps the most commonly used test question is the age-old multiple-choice question, with a stem and then a selection of choices. There are good ways to write these questions that will make the questions more valid. Carjuzaa and Kellough (2017) recommend the following:

- The stem should state a single and specific point.
- The item should be expressed in a positive form.
- Every item should be grammatically consistent.
- The stem should not include clues to the correct alternative.
- Incorrect responses (distractors) should be plausible and related to the same concept as the correct alternative. (pp. 362–63)

Additionally, there should be only one correct or best response. Here is a bad example for a multiple-choice question:

Chapter 7

Which of the following presidents is not considered a founding father of our nation?

a. George Washington
b. Pat Nixon
c. Thomas Jefferson
d. John Adams

It's pretty obvious that Pat Nixon stands out. Does this really help students learn the meaning of "founding father"? How many thirteen-year-olds have even heard of Pat Nixon?

A better example for a multiple-choice answer:

The square root of 64 is

a. 6
b. 8
c. 4
d. 2

There is only one right answer, 8. Should the possible responses be in order, 2, 4, 6, 8? Yes, it would guide the test taker better.

What we call fill-in-the-blank questions are also called completion questions. These questions have to be clear enough for only one correct answer. If multiple answers are possible, students should be made aware of that in the directions.

Examples of questions with multiple and just one possible completion answer:

_____ was considered a founding father in American history.

_____ was the second president of the United States.

Is a test with matching very useful in assessing student learning? It might be a way to assess definitions and lower-level, basic learning. Matching is often used when a lot of material needs to be assessed quickly. Students seem to like this type of assessment.

1. el gato_____   a. the bird
2. el perro_____   b. the hen
3. el pato_____   c. the horse
4. la gallina_____   d. the rabbit

5. el caballo_____   e. the dog
　　　　　　　　　　　f. the cat
　　　　　　　　　　　g. the duck

Of course, the big hint when writing this type of assessment is to have more possible answers than words or phrases to match.

Should students be writing short-answer responses and essays as test assessments? Essays can demonstrate higher-order thinking, and that's a good thing. The downside is that essay questions take so much more time to read and grade. If using essay questions, consider including a checklist or rubric for students to follow when writing. With specific guidelines, students can write better essays, and your grading becomes easier. Let students know ahead of time if or how much spelling, grammar, and usage count.

Note the differences between the following two questions. Which would *you* rather answer?

a. Write a three-paragraph essay about the founding fathers of the United States.
b. Write a three-paragraph essay about the concept of the founding fathers of the United States. For full credit, list three of the men who are considered to be in this group. Write enough about each of the three to explain how they fit into the founding fathers group. Include the significance of the contributions of this group of men.

Successful teachers know that how they write the test will have an effect on the students' scores. A poorly written test does little to determine what was learned by the students and is extremely frustrating for them. In today's age of teacher accountability, parents expect high-quality, valid, and reliable tests from their children's teachers.

TURNING ASSESSMENTS INTO GRADES

In my work with student teachers, I have seen many who say that they know how to assess student learning but are clueless about how to grade students. Turning assessments into grades should be a simple, straightforward procedure. For example, turning a rubric into a grade is very clear. Each performance indicator box has a number assigned to it. If there are six criteria and each one can be assessed for one to five points, then a score of 30 is possible. Turn this score into a grade as follows:

A = 90–100 percent; 27–30 points
B = 80–89 percent; 24–26 points

C = 70–79 percent; 21–25 points
D = 60–69 percent; 18–20 points
F = 0–59 percent; 0–17 points

Now, how does this one-letter grade count toward a nine-week or semester grade? The creation of a grading system must be done within the guidelines of the school. In some schools, the administration sets the percentage cutoffs for letter grades. In other schools, perhaps only numeric averages are the "grades" sent home to families. A third option for distributing assessment data is verbal descriptors. A verbal descriptor is an achievement-level classification, such as advanced, proficient, basic, or below basic (Popham, 2011). Verbal descriptors are used for standards-based report cards, where the assessments support mastery of each standard or learning goal.

When I got my first teaching job, I knew how to grade tests and papers but not how to turn those into final grades. The thought of using a percentage system, such as 35 percent of the semester grade based on tests, 25 percent on quizzes, 20 percent on homework, and 20 percent on special projects, seemed like a puzzle only a PhD in statistics could master. If the teacher can't explain the grading system to students, parents, and the principal, the system won't be a successful one.

Fortunately for me, a caring teacher next door introduced me to total point grading, and it saved my life with regard to turning assessments into final grades. The beauty of the total point system is that it is usable for any grade level and every type of assignment. Here is how it works.

Every assignment has a point value. I repeat, *every* assignment, quiz, test, project, or even participation has a point value. Students earn points, and then their points are divided by the total points possible. This yields a percentage. The percentage is then given a letter grade based on the teacher's (or school's) policies.

Elementary teachers often quickly review students' work for completion, giving students a star, a check, or a minus. How does one average six stars, five checks, and two minuses? Here's how. Instead of stars, make those quick checks worth five points. A check is worth three, and a minus is worth zero. Now, the student has earned 45 points for homework quick checks. Sixty-five points were available. The student has earned 45/65, which is 69 percent for homework completion. On my basic scale, that's an F. The student and the parents are probably surprised by this F, when they saw that their student was getting stars. Eliminate the star, check, and minus system, and implement points. It's clearer! Remind students, and maybe even parents, that 3/5 is 60 percent, and that's failing.

Now, let's turn a lot of grades into a final grade with the total point grading system.

In this class, your nine-week grade is based on how many points you earn. You earn points as follows:

- Homework and short assignments: 5 to 15 points each, approximately one grade per week
- Quizzes: 15 to 25 points
- Chapter tests: 50 to 125 points
- One project or speech: 70 points

To compute your grade on any day of the grading period, add up your points earned and divide by the total! Here's an example:

- Homework and short assignments: 5/5, 7/10, 12/12, 0/5, 8/10, 13/15, 12/12, 15/15 = 72 points earned out of 84 possible
- Quizzes: 15/15, 21/25, 13/15, 18/25, 16/20 = 83 points earned out of 100 possible
- Chapter tests: 45/50, 88/100, 86/100 = 219 earned out of 250 possible
- One project or speech: 65/70 = 65 points earned out of 70 possible
- Total points earned by student = 439
- Total points possible = 504
- Percentage = 439/504 = 87 percent
- On the 90, 80, 70, 60 percent scale, this is a clear B.

For the statistically inclined, homework and assignments are worth 16 percent (84 points divided by the total of 504). Chapter tests are worth 50 percent. The teacher need not be a rocket scientist to use total point grading.

An advantage to this system is that the teacher does not need to know how many assignments will be in the grading period. If there are snow days, there is no need to worry about having four chapter tests in that nine weeks—just average the points on the chapter tests that were given.

Another advantage is that this system works so well on any spreadsheet or online grading platform. If the grading platform uses total points, then both students and parents can see progress on a daily basis. It is so simple that even a principal should be able to understand the system.

Does everything need to be graded, and how does a teacher have time to grade? Students need feedback on everything they do. Some feedback is verbal/informal. Other times, students can check their own work, viewing the answers on the classroom screen. Online programs can be used by students to verify their answers, with the results sent directly to the teacher's computer. (It's still private because only the teacher sees the results.)

What are some other caveats about grading that successful teachers know?

1. A student's grades should be known only to the student and his or her parents or guardians.
2. Teachers should not read grades aloud.
3. Students should not grade other students' papers for a final grade. Students may peer-edit or check for corrections, but teachers assign grades.
4. Teachers must understand online grading systems well enough to explain them to students and their families.
5. Grading should be as objective as possible. It is not best practice to set up a grading scale and then give students grades based on your opinion or their attitude.
6. Grades are a big deal. When it comes time to name a high school valedictorian, the students' grade point averages are a huge deal. College entrance remains a competitive process, and grades contribute to college selectivity.

WHEN AND HOW TO SHARE ASSESSMENT DATA

Research says that teachers spend up to 30 percent of classroom time in assessment-related functions (Stronge, Grant, & Xu, 2017). Is this too much? Will parents ask why? It is important to be able to explain to parents that significant gains in student academic achievement are made when assessments and instruction are integrated. In other words, we do testing for learning and not just testing of learning.

Successful teachers explain vocabulary to parents/families so they understand. It's certainly OK, and actually recommended, to explain to parents that your tests are teacher made to assess whether students have met objectives. Of course, if a big project or speech is a large percentage of a final grade, you can explain that not all tests are paper and pencil. Do parents want to know about validity and reliability? Yes, some do. Others just want to know whether their student is passing and whether the test was important. Know your parent audience.

There are some very practical ways of sharing assessment and grading information. Parent/teacher conferences are one example. Successful teachers have learned that a good way to open a parent conference is to show samples of the students' work. I vividly remember an awkward parent conference where a mother came into the conference complaining loudly about her son's D in my sophomore class. She said she couldn't understand how he could be getting a D. I pulled his folder, showed her three chapter exams with grades of C-, D, and F. She then exclaimed, "Why, I can't even read his writing." "Neither can I," I replied. She calmed down, and we discussed ways to help her son with his issues.

What does the teacher share about classwide results or grade-level results? This type of assessment reporting is usually done for the principal in response to his or her need for further reporting to the district administration. Standardized test scores are an example. Some principals will need reading performance scores or semester grades for a class. Again, this data is shared with administrators. When a parent asks "Where does my child stand with regard to his or her class?" teachers have to answer carefully. We don't say "Well, his latest grades put him 15th out of 30 for math skills." Overall ranges may be shared: "Second-grade students fall into the 80th percentile districtwide, and your son has scored at the 85th percentile." Of course, then you have to explain percentiles.

Should we ask students to assess their own learning? Definitely, and in a variety of ways. Students can complete a rubric for how they completed a task. They can self-assess to guide their own goal setting. Should students assess their teachers, as college students do each semester? Even young children can be asked very simple evaluative questions, such as:

I learn a lot in this class.   yes or no
I like reading the books in this class. yes or no

Should we ask parents to assess their child's learning? Should parents assess their child's teacher's performance? The school's performance? Actually, all three of these assessments are done in some schools. Parent surveys do provide feedback to the teachers and administrators. A parent survey might look like the following:

On a scale of 1 to 3, where 3 indicates very pleased, are you pleased with . . .

1. Your child's progress with reading?
2. The amount of work your child is doing?
3. The communication from the child's teacher?

How valid are parent responses? Parents are not teaching experts. They may not understand developmental readiness and think that their child should be succeeding much more quickly. It can be helpful to look for patterns in parent surveys when requesting feedback.

PROGRAM AND SCHOOLWIDE ASSESSMENTS

Teachers often sit in the workroom (lounge) and complain about not having input into decisions made about the school. They may want new books or a new math curriculum, but complaining to each other about these programs won't make them happen. Successful teachers know that they can have input on program and schoolwide changes by using assessments as data.

Why are programs assessed? In the simplest of terms, we assess to see whether a program should be continued—to see if it is working. We assess for improvements. To be an accredited institution, assessments of programs are essential.

Stakeholders play an increased role in program assessment because administrators seek input from teachers and parents. Technology has made data gathering so much easier. Think about a quick online survey to teachers and parents as opposed to the cost and inconvenience of sending out a paper survey.

What kinds of assessments are needed to implement change or improvements? It depends on the goals. Once the issue is defined, then an assessment can be designed. The following are examples of program review questions and possible assessments of them:

1. Issue: After a schoolwide field trip, the teachers and administrators need to decide whether the field trip should be repeated next year.

    Assessment: Ask teachers to complete a survey of importance of the trip, value of the costs and time, and other issues.

2. Issue: A small, private school that offers prekindergarten through fourth grade is considering adding fifth and sixth grades.

    Assessment: To gather data, survey the parents about their interest in fifth and sixth grades. Determine the potential enrollment numbers for the additional two grades.

3. Issue: The school is considering a very expensive new math curriculum.

    Assessment: How have the standardized test scores of the past five years compared to the state's scores?

4. Issue: The purchase of 500 laptops could allow each student to have a laptop to use all day.

    Assessment: Ask teachers what they would do with laptops in their classrooms. What specific activities could teachers do with laptops that they can't do now?

Successful teachers feel that they are not only a part of a change but they are the impetus for the change. Too often, change is something that comes from the top administration and is simply placed upon teachers. Teachers don't like surprises and changes that are placed upon them. With better information about assessments, teachers can work for program and school improvement.

KEYS FOR SUCCESS

1. Successful teachers assess their students' learning informally and continually. They know when their students are prepared for a final assessment.
2. Successful teachers use a variety of assessments, not just tests.
3. Successful teachers choose well-written published tests that accompany their textbooks, or they write their own tests with several types of questions.
4. Successful teachers know how to implement usable, valid grading systems.
5. Successful teachers can explain grading to students, parents, and administrators.
6. Successful teachers are involved in assessments of programs at their schools. They know that they can be advocates for important changes and improvements.

Chapter Eight

Meet the Needs of All Students

> Successful teachers recognize and accept the differences among students, striving to meet their academic needs.

I heard Steve Sroka speak at a national conference. He began his keynote address by showing his third-grade report card on the big screen. On the report card, his teacher had written to his parents, "You need to get help for your son, as he is retarted." Interestingly, his third-grade teacher did not spell retarded correctly. Steve went on to become a teacher and a National Teacher Hall of Fame award winner and to earn a PhD (for more information, see www.drstephensroka.com). Times have changed dramatically since Steve Sroka was in elementary school.

In the late 1990s, I was supervising a student teacher in a third-grade classroom. I couldn't help but notice a boy sitting in a corner with a sewing machine on his desk. He did not participate at all in the language arts lesson taught by the student teacher nor did the regular classroom teacher work with the child during the hour of my observation. Immediately after the lesson, I asked about the boy.

"Oh," responded the student teacher, "he doesn't participate because he can't read. He is very good with his hands, and he likes to sew and put things together. The teacher keeps him busy with projects." As a professional educator, I had a meltdown. Trying to keep my voice calm and realizing that student teachers are guests in the classrooms where they worked, I still had to discuss this issue. "This student must get an intervention, *now*! He must get the help he needs to develop literacy. This can't wait!"

No teacher should ever allow a student to sit in the corner of a classroom and not learn. This is an extreme example that exemplifies why the movement to meet the needs of all students emerged and is not going away. The language used for children with special needs has changed, as has how teachers strive to meet the needs of students. Virtually every teacher job candidate will be asked how he or she meets the needs of all students in the classroom. Practicing teachers are expected to serve all students with equity and to differentiate instruction for individuals.

Devoting only a chapter to meeting the needs of all students will barely scratch the surface of the big issues, but successful teachers know that they must accept all the students who come into their classrooms. After acceptance comes teaching.

This chapter will look at some aspects of the diversity of students, teaching students with special needs, including gifted students, and teaching English language learners. Differentiation is woven in to each segment.

STUDENT DIVERSITY

All teacher education students in the United States take at least one course dedicated to student diversity or multicultural education. Different courses have varying standards and topics. Many courses stress having students look at the big questions surrounding the diversity of students, including:

1. What is discrimination, and how have schools perpetuated discrimination in the past?
2. Is racism persistent in US schools?
3. Who are the low socioeconomic students, and does socioeconomic status influence students' school experience?
4. What are the immigration trends in the United States?
5. What are the educational issues for immigrant children, especially illegal immigrant children in the schools?
6. Should/how should teachers integrate students' cultural backgrounds into their classrooms?
7. What does it mean to affirm the diversity of students?
8. How can teachers raise their expectations of all students regardless of students' backgrounds?
9. How can teachers raise students' expectations for their learning and success?
10. How do teachers promote socially just practices in classrooms? Should this be a part of the curriculum?
11. What does it mean to give children an "equal" education?
12. What are the challenges of teaching demographically diverse students in today's schools?

Faculties in colleges of teacher education hope that their programs of coursework and field experiences prepare teachers to work with and succeed with all students. Sonia Nieto (2013) has written, "Teachers of *all* backgrounds are responsible for teaching *all* students effectively; however, without personal or professional experience with diversity, miscommunication, mistrust, and discomfort between teachers and students of different backgrounds are common" (p. 17).

In her book *Finding Joy in Students of Diverse Backgrounds*, Nieto (2013) stresses the value of in-service professional development, mentoring, induction programs, and teacher collaboration to support the work of teachers as they cope with the expectations of teaching all students. Much of the aforementioned book includes the personal stories of teachers who are not only coping with the many diversities of their classrooms but also thriving in that work. There are no simple answers nor are there some teaching tricks that always work with students of diverse backgrounds.

Although not fast and simple answers, there are some guiding principles that help teachers with teaching to all. Teachers must recognize their own backgrounds and experiences, take a look at what "baggage" they may bring to their work, and then focus on what Nieto (2013) calls teaching as "an ethical endeavor" (p. 127). Teachers who do this recognize that teaching is about preparing good people, people who go out into the world later in life and contribute.

It can be said that successful teachers are dreamers. They not only dream for themselves, but they promote dreaming for a better future by their students. Of course, to make dreams come true, teachers have to impress upon their students the importance of education. It's easy for a student to say "I want to be a doctor or an engineer." The math and science that professionals in these fields need begins in kindergarten. A teacher has to get students to dream and get them to learn the skills that will make the dream possible.

Teachers who recognize the importance of students' cultures can go a step further and ensure that students are reading literature reflective of those cultures. Teachers can become students' advocates, making sure that all students and their parents are aware of gifted classes, tutoring services, and other opportunities that families can use to their advantage. Good communication with families is always important.

Smith, Frey, Pumpian, and Fisher (2017) wrote that "What it means for schools to be fair has changed over the decades" (p. 1). It wasn't that long ago that girls were discouraged from advanced science classes in high schools or that persons of color were discouraged by their guidance counselors from applying to four-year colleges. Successful teachers strive to offer opportunities to all of their students and by doing so will have successful students.

TEACHING STUDENTS WITH SPECIAL NEEDS

There is a recurring myth about teachers that both parents and administrators may believe. The myth is that a good teacher should be able to handle anything or anyone in the classroom without outside help. When it comes to teaching students with special needs, this is indeed a myth. No teacher can know everything about all areas of special needs nor can any one teacher work with the most severe cases in a regular classroom with no assistance. What should the expectations be for a teacher who is not certificated/endorsed in special education within the regular classroom?

All teachers who are prepared in accredited college programs take at least one course in teaching students with exceptionalities. In this course, they generally learn the vocabulary for special education, the federal and state laws governing least restrictive environment, and basic principles for working with children identified with special needs.

Once teachers are employed, I recommend that they keep at least a couple of textbooks on special education in their professional library and refer to them often (see, for example, Billingsley, Brownell, Israel, & Kamman, 2013; Martin & Hauth, 2015). When faced with a new or challenging situation, always go to a mentor, a department chair, or an administrator to get more information. Ask a lot of questions and seek the necessary help.

The Council for Exceptional Children (www.cec.sped.org) is a site that every teacher needs to read frequently. Not just for teachers of special education but for all teachers, this site provides excellent articles and resources. The section called Tool of the Week is a very practical area of the website, providing timely suggestions and useful downloads—all free (https://tooloftheweek.org/hows-your-co-teaching).

Some Basic Principles

One guiding principle for regular education teachers who work with special needs students is to be familiar with the school's special education policies. In many schools, there are pull-out programs for students, whereas in other schools, there is more mainstreaming, with special education teachers working side by side with the classroom teacher for all or part of the day. Another model is that of the special education teacher being a case worker. The case worker provides the classroom teacher with the student's background, individualized education plan (IEP), and suggestions for teaching, but the classroom teacher provides the instruction.

Assessment is a huge part of special education, and teachers need to know the requirements of students with special needs for in-class and standardized testing. Always ask about the accommodations required for each student and how those accommodations will be administered. Who will proctor standardized tests for your students if testing is done outside of the classroom? Who else will be involved in preparing the students for the exams?

Sometimes a rearrangement of the classroom is needed to accommodate students. One teacher had to make room for a hospital bed in her elementary classroom to accommodate a student. Another had to make pathways in her room to accommodate a blind student. Many students, especially those on the autism spectrum, want and need personal space. Placing these students at tables, with their backpacks slung over their chairs, is not going to be conducive to their learning. Having individual desks for students can optimize concentration and peace of mind for students—even young ones. Students need a place for everything and everything in its place.

Here is an example of what *not* to do. In an elementary school, teachers were asked to pair up their classrooms to "differentiate instruction." So every time a lesson was taught, forty-two young children sat on the floor for the "lesson." Next, the forty-two students were divided into their groups and went to tables for group work and practice. Two classroom teachers, a paraprofessional and a special education teacher floated among the groups to assist students—to differentiate instruction. A student teacher often assisted.

The problems with this scenario included the fact that young children who sat in the back of the room on the floor couldn't see the screen or whiteboard. The movement of two groups of classes into one group of forty-two was time consuming and chaotic, no matter what the teachers did to make a routine. With no desks for individual students, these eight-year-olds were always packing up their materials and lugging their backpacks. They needed desks and private space, but somewhere along the history of education, their administrators determined that desks were "bad" and tables for group work were "good." For optimal learning, consider classroom space issues.

Collaboration and communication are huge issues when teachers work together, and especially so when working with special educators. If possible, sit down with coteachers and outline expectations. Have the special education teachers clarify when they will be in the classroom and when they will have conference time alone with the regular teacher. If an issue arises, don't let it fester for a long time. Discuss issues immediately.

The following are worst-case scenarios related to me by former graduate students who were practicing teachers. Think about each scenario and what you would have done to improve the situation or to report it to someone who could help.

1. The special education teacher is in the classroom of a middle-grades teacher for the prescribed time. He sits at the teacher's desk and completes paperwork and forms for the students in the room as well as other students. He leaves lengthy reports for the teacher about what

she should do for her special needs students. When asked why he isn't assisting with instruction or student behavior, he replies, "I'm so busy with paperwork that if I don't spend my time doing it in your classroom, my work won't be done. I don't have time to teach or monitor behavior. If *you* would follow my outlines with these students, their test scores should go up." Ouch!

2. One-third of a class has been identified as English language learners, one-third qualify for some special education interventions, and the remaining third are not identified with any special needs. A first-year teacher is given the classroom. She is told that special education teachers become available about the third week of the school year and are not available the last month of the school year because of their need to complete files and paperwork. There will be no ELL specialist assigned to the class, but the ELL teacher will visit the school two days a week to answer questions and translate parent newsletters into Spanish. (This teacher was told at the end of the year that she would receive a "needs improvement" evaluation because she didn't have high test scores. She resigned and went to work for a private school.)

3. A special education teacher is in the classroom for two-thirds of the day. She makes negative remarks to both her students and students who are not receiving accommodations. She does not follow the established classroom guidelines for student behavior and is actually more of a distraction than a help. When approached by the classroom teacher privately about expectations, the special educator replies, "Look, you get me or you get no one. I know what I'm doing."

For each of these three scenarios, the classroom teacher must know where to turn for help. The school should have a chain of command for conflicts. If so, follow it. If there are no procedures in place, consider talking to a mentor teacher or department chair. Discuss the issue, and ask the mentor/chair to join a conversation. Then, sit down with the mentor and special educator to review expectations. If a conversation does not go well or if no changes happen, go to the next administrator, either a special education director or the building principal. What does one do if the principal is not helpful? Try your professional association/union representative.

Succeeding with Special Needs Students

It can be very rewarding to work with students with special needs. These students need frequent opportunities for success and frequent responses to their work, both academic and behavioral. Many teachers report that they adapt the interventions suggested by special educators and use them for all students. These interventions are generally very effective teaching strategies.

The technology provided for students with special needs often provides teachers with insights about how to use technology for all students. Interactive whiteboards and clickers support learning for all students while keeping students engaged. Sometimes, the assistive technologies for students with special needs can be very low tech. Examples include pencil and pen grips, highlighters, sticky notes, and paper with larger spaces between lines (Billingsley et al., 2013, p. 208).

A tried-and-true strategy for students with limited attention spans is to divide their work into smaller, more doable chunks. One teacher would cut up a worksheet for a student, telling him that when he finished his work, she would check back with him. He needed this constant attention and feedback. He would do one-fourth of a worksheet easily but was overwhelmed when he saw the whole worksheet and would shut down, not attempting anything. She also photocopied some pages of the book so that she could cut his reading assignments in chunks as well.

A large part of succeeding with students with special needs is learning how to advocate for them. As a classroom teacher, you can't do everything for the child nor should you be expected to do everything. However, identifying students who may need help and advocating for them may be the teacher's best way to serve students. Because the identification process varies state to state and district to district, know the procedures for recommending a student for evaluation for special help. Do not start with the parents. Follow your school's procedures for recommendations and interventions.

Practicing teachers say that getting help for their students with special needs has become much easier than in the past. They report that special educators are the lifesavers for students in their classrooms and for them. The next question becomes, "What should teachers do about the students with learning issues and behavioral issues who are not identified as having special needs and are not getting additional services?" There are indeed many students in these categories. Some parents refuse to have their children tested for special needs and want the teacher to "do a better job by individualizing instruction."

Middle and high school teachers often lament that students' issues went undiagnosed in elementary school, leaving them with students who are years behind academically. It is genuinely hard to fix holes in students' academic careers. Imagine getting students in 11th-grade English who read at a second-grade level. Then, imagine having to get them to pass a standardized test and write a term paper. Remember, your reemployment may be partially based on their test scores too. It is a challenge. Early intervention does help tremendously, but special educators are trained to work with students in middle and high schools. Use their expertise, and don't hesitate to ask for help. As a college professor, I see more and more of my students applying for and receiving accommodations to help them succeed academically.

For older students, accommodations can be more time for testing, having a text that they can listen to instead of read, or having lecture notes provided before the class. Older students may need a copy of the PowerPoints rather than just viewing them in class. Personalized tutors can share notes or spend time outside of class reviewing with the student. I know of one high school student who had a deaf interpreter attend all of his classes with him, and she reviewed material at least one hour a day one-on-one. The school district hired her full-time to serve this student for all four years of his high school attendance.

To summarize, a teacher in a regular education classroom may have a large number of special needs students in the room, with or without the assistance of special educators. Getting help for the students remains a primary consideration. Following school policies and procedures is critical for success when working with other educators in the classroom. Communication is important, as is knowing when to turn to someone else for help. If issues arise, document everything about both the students and their special educators. It is much more convincing to go to a director or department chair with a list of dates, times, and observable behaviors than to go to a meeting and say "My coteacher is not doing her job."

Continue to learn about today's students and their needs. More and more research becomes available each year about learning needs and behavioral issues. Keep reading professional journals, online materials, and books. Much has changed since the days when a teacher could write to parents and tell them that their son was retarded. We all hope that the future holds even more positive changes.

Gifted Students and Their Special Needs

Are gifted students categorized as students with special needs? Generally, yes, they are because they do have unique needs. I once heard a conference speaker say that gifted students are often learning the least in our schools because so little attention is given to their needs. It's food for thought. What can teachers do to ensure a fair and meaningful education for their gifted students?

The Council for Exceptional Children (CEC) has a division designed to provide resources for those teaching gifted children (http://cectag.com/). Their publications include the *Journal for the Education of the Gifted*. Additionally, a quick online search will yield a multitude of books with strategies for teaching gifted children in all classrooms. As with any other issue in education, a teacher can always find resources and read for ideas.

What are some basic guidelines for what to do and not to do with your gifted students?

To do:

1. Know how your district/school identifies gifted students for support.
2. Find out what is available in your school or district for support. Are there gifted teachers who can come in to your room or pull out some students?
3. Plan to support these students with differentiated assignments and supplemental materials.
4. Work closely with parents regarding communication about the unique skills of the student and how you are meeting the student's needs.
5. Find out whether your district has agreements with nearby colleges for workshops and classes for your students.
6. Protect these students from bullying by their peers.
7. Recognize that a gifted student may have unique skills in one or more subjects but not all. (A student may be strong in math but not in language arts.)
8. Strive to provide support for students who are talented in music and art, especially if your school has limited programs.
9. Be aware that gifted students may have unique social and emotional reactions to other students. Help with social/emotional skills may be needed. (Think about the character of Sheldon on the TV show *The Big Bang Theory*.)
10. Having access to technology may be a big help for your students.
11. These students may not respond well to sharing a table all day in the classroom. They may need considerable personal space, at least a private desk where they can keep their things. (Again, this is actually good advice for most students.)

Not to do:

1. A gifted student should not just be given more to do. A student will realize that more work is just more work and may shut down.
2. The gifted students should not spend large amounts of their extra time tutoring weaker students. They are not teachers and shouldn't have to tutor others.
3. Do not seat these students all together in your room. Mixed seating and grouping can be beneficial.
4. Be aware of your comments to gifted students, especially in front of the whole class. Do not single these students out or make a comment such as "Oh, you should have known that."
5. Be aware that some gifted students are very quiet and they may not want to shout out answers or compete in classroom games. Don't force them to do so.

As with other students with special needs, getting to know the gifted students is important. Some students may appear gifted because their parents read a lot to them or took them on exciting trips as young children. Their vocabulary may make them appear "super" smart. Students from higher socioeconomic levels may appear advanced compared to their peers, but truly gifted students are from all walks of life and all socioeconomic levels.

Gifted students may develop a mindset that they are so smart that they don't have to work hard to learn. When they reach a level of learning that isn't instant, they may shut down. They may not want to practice or study because they feel that they should be learning instantly. Carol Dweck's (2007) book, *Mindset*, provides much insight into this area of learning. Learning to learn and learning to study are truly important skills that all students need to learn, as is humility.

Some parents come to their child's teachers and say that their child is misbehaving because he or she is bored and gifted. This may be true in some cases, but many times, students who have limited attention spans and don't want to work on material that they don't find immediately engaging just claim to be bored. If a student who is getting 100 percent on every assignment and is paying attention says that he or she is bored, then there might be an issue worth investigating.

Many courses have been "watered down" to meet the needs of the general student, and these courses may indeed bore students. Getting students into the appropriate middle and secondary courses that meet their needs is important. High schools in Georgia allow joint enrollment with area colleges for a program called Dual Enrollment, formerly called Move On When Ready. Students can finish high school with as much as two years' worth of college credit. More school systems may implement similar programs in the future.

TEACHING ENGLISH LANGUAGE LEARNERS (ELLS)

Anyone who has traveled in a foreign country knows the frustration of not being able to communicate clearly with the native speakers in that country. Now, imagine being a child or adolescent in a classroom and not being able to understand or speak to the teacher and the majority of your peers. Teachers want to help but often don't know where to start to assist the English language learners in their classes. Those teachers who have had the opportunity to take methods of teaching English as a Second Language (ESOL) or TEFL (Teaching English as a Foreign Language) courses have the background to work successfully with these students.

Some teachers who have worked with ELLs say that the strategies and methods for teaching these students in a regular classroom are the same as "just good teaching." An example might be the use of procedures and routines. Every student, including those learning English, can benefit from predictable routines in the classroom. Routines save time and improve classroom behavior.

The use of visuals is good teaching in any classroom, especially the classroom with ELLs. Signage helps all students—especially with pictures and language. The word "realia" refers to real things—tangible, concrete objects. If a teacher is teaching about fruits and vegetables, bringing in fruits and vegetables will help students learn the language by seeing the realia. Using plastic fruits works too, but real ones that are eaten as part of the lesson are more fun. Think about advanced science classes in high school. What types of visuals and realia would make difficult material more comprehensible?

Anything that a teacher can do to organize a lesson beforehand will also help the ELLs. Called advance organizers by Ausabel (as cited in Herrell & Jordan, 2004, p. 33), they can vary from a picture to Venn diagrams or adding technology to clarify the day's lesson from the very beginning. The more organized the teacher, the better the students can understand the concepts being taught while learning the language.

Vocabulary is critically important for those learning English in the regular classroom setting. Teaching students how to make flashcards for vocabulary is a good learning strategy. In her book, *Teaching Unprepared Students*, Gabriel (2008) suggested having college students make flashcards that include drawings on one side of the cards. If this is a recommended strategy for college students, it is definitely appropriate for students in K–12.

All teachers should already be teachers of reading. Language acquisition and reading go hand in hand. When learning a language, students begin to understand, to speak, to read, and to write. Some argue that the skills are not learned in order and that reading, or at least recognizing words, can be much easier for students than speaking. While teaching Chinese students (in China), I discovered that they were great writers in English even when their spoken English was much weaker. All teachers can reinforce reading in English with printed signs in the room and posted procedures for all activities.

When creating opportunities for all of our students to be highly engaged, using songs and games can help. I still remember learning the definition of a circle, sung to the tune of "Jingle Bells." I think it was in my second year of high school too. Don't overlook any idea that helps students to use language—rhymes, songs, tongue twisters, or games with lots of words. Most of us remember learning multiples of numbers by playing around the world. Students stand in a circle and count, inserting a fun word for multiples of a chosen number—one, two, RED, four, five, RED.

Moving beyond the "just good teaching" ideas, Herrell and Jordan (2004) recommended that teachers understand language acquisition as a basis for teaching students who are English language learners. Those who teach language know that students need comprehensible input—"material presented in a manner that leads to the student's understanding of the content" (Herrell & Jordan, 2004, p. 5). Teachers of language strive to reduce the anxiety levels of students because stress overload can reduce learning and being the nonnative speakers of English in the class is already stressful. Knowledge of English phonetics and grammar helps a teacher to teach the language while teaching the subject content.

I used to teach a course titled Spanish for Teachers. I began the course with the Spanish alphabet, stressing the vowels *a*, *e*, *i*, *o*, and *u*. In Spanish, the letter *e* has the long *a* sound, and the letter *i* has the long *e* sound of English. Imagine the confusion when an elementary teacher is teaching spelling to native speakers of Spanish and the teacher says it's an *a* and the student is hearing *e* or it's an *e* and the student is hearing *i*. Even a bit of phonics can help when teaching those learning English as a second language from Spanish. Of course, no teacher can know the phonics of every language the students in her room speak.

Helena Curtain and Carol Ann Dahlberg (2016), noted authors in the field of world language instruction, have long espoused the value of connecting language to content.

> Content-related instruction supports what we know about how the brain makes connections and how learning takes place. Students are actively engaged in constructing meaning and making sense of the interesting world presented to them through the vehicle of the target [English] language. (p. 227)

When native speakers of English are learning to measure, for example, they are learning vocabulary that they did not know previously. The words and skills of measuring are new to all the students in the class, and the ELLs will be learning the content as well as the language. The visuals and actions of measuring will assist the learners greatly. Again, making learning visual, with realia to support vocabulary, provides opportunities for learning language and content.

Connecting language to culture is a standard of teaching all foreign/world languages. When working with English language learners in any classroom, acceptance of their culture is important. Additionally, these students are learning both school and societal culture in the classroom.

Third-culture kids may have even greater challenges with regard to navigating the school environment. A third-culture kid is one whose home country, school culture, and societal culture are all different. For example, a student from Korea who lives in China with his or her parents and attends an American international school has to navigate three cultures and languages—Korean at home, English at school, and Chinese when out in the public community. The teacher's awareness of these issues is helpful for bridging the gaps for these students.

Above all, do not think that a lack of second or third language skill is indicative of low intellectual ability. When traveling in Germany, I was hosted by a family with a four-year-old daughter. I played a simple card game with her. At one point, she stopped playing and ran to her mother. The sweet little girl wanted to know what was wrong with me because I could count to only ten and couldn't make a sentence. The little girl wanted to help me because she considered me a nice adult but one who was apparently quite mentally challenged. Her mother explained that it was a language issue and that I was quite normal mentally. This is a lesson for all teachers to remember when teaching English language learners.

KEYS FOR SUCCESS

1. Successful teachers accept the diverse backgrounds of students who enter their classes and strive to make all students successful.
2. Successful teachers continue to learn about diversity and multicultural education.
3. Successful teachers work to identify the special needs of students and to get additional help and support for those students.
4. Successful teachers seek and accept help for their students with special needs and language needs.
5. Successful teachers maintain positive communication with specialist teachers, administrators, and parents regarding the needs of students.
6. Successful teachers read widely—books, professional journals, and online resources. They read to stay informed about meeting students' needs. Something has been published about virtually every aspect of student diversity, special education, and language learning, with more research appearing every day.

Chapter Nine

Communicate with All Stakeholders

> Successful teachers know that what they say may be on Facebook in a matter of seconds.

A wise teacher once said to a parent, "I won't believe everything I hear from your child about you if you don't believe everything your child says about me." I used to advise student teachers to never say anything in class that would be embarrassing if it appeared on the front page of the local newspaper the next day. Of course, with social media, I now advise student teachers that anything they say might be quoted by a student on social media instantly. I also advise all teachers to never say anything to a student in class that they wouldn't say if an administrator were in the room conducting a formal evaluation. Other cautionary advice might include:

1. Sarcasm is not a good way to communicate. Yes, today's students are themselves sarcastic, but teachers have to be above sarcasm.
2. Empty threats simply should not be spoken. A teacher should not say, "Stop that or I'll throw you out the window" or "Move your leg, or I'll break it." Students can twist this into an abusive threat. (Both of these examples were given to me by teachers who said them and were proud of their lines!)
3. Teachers should not say anything that they would not want their own child's teacher to say to their child. It's like the Golden Rule—do unto others as you would have them do unto you.
4. Do not yell. There are much better ways to get students' attention and to communicate with them. Lowering your voice works wonderfully. You may yell if the school is on fire or a student is in true danger.
5. Keep communications with students as private as possible, whether it's about grades, behavior, or praise.

Chapter 9

COMMUNICATION WITH PARENTS AND FAMILIES

Throughout this chapter and this book, the words *parents* and *families* are used interchangeably. Teachers must be cautious about the language used in any communication. It is best to follow the practice of the culture of the school where you work. Many educators advocate the phrase "families and guardians" when sending out newsletters and notes. Others may say "families and caregivers." Of course, some parents feel slighted if the word parent isn't used! Ask your colleagues about the most acceptable phrasing in your school's culture.

Read the following scenarios, and ask yourself whether you should communicate with the parents/family about the incident and, if so, how you should communicate.

1. You have been informed that Susan has the mumps and will miss a week of school.
2. Logan cheated on a chapter test.
3. Morgan stole lunch money.
4. Jerry called Stephanie a cow just as the bell rang.
5. Jerry called Stephanie a much worse name.
6. Jose scored the winning touchdown at the football game.
7. After having a nine-week average of 72 percent, Bethany received a 92 percent on a major assignment.
8. Ray told you that his parents are divorcing.
9. Ray told you that his dad hit him hard enough to split his lip.
10. Katie is a continual tattler. She comes to you at least four times a day to report on other students.

For these, and the myriad of other examples of student behaviors, ask yourself, "If my child did this, would I want to hear from the teacher?" And how would you want to hear from the teacher? Of course, teachers should contact parents for exceptional positive incidents as well as negative ones. Some things must be reported immediately to school administration, such as a student's report of being hit. The teacher should never contact parents when school policy for reporting of abuse must be followed.

Ways of Communicating

We all remember the days when the teacher would send notes home to parents with students as messengers. This is one way to communicate, but don't count on the note getting home, unless of course the highly reliable student is taking home a positive note. Consider the school culture when deciding how to communicate. In some schools, paper notes and newsletters still work great.

E-mail is now considered mainstream communication. However, there are confidentiality issues with the use of e-mail. If used, it is best to find out where to send the e-mail messages at the beginning of the year. Who is the child's parent, guardian, or family member responsible for the student? Which parent gets the communication in a divorce? Some divorce decrees stipulate that only one parent will receive school-related information. Some parents still don't use e-mail or simply don't want you to communicate with them this way. In the initial parent letter home, ask about preferred communication.

Should you text parents? Many teachers are doing this, but getting the parent's permission is a good idea before implementing texting as a means of communication. If you text from a personal phone, be prepared for a mountain of texts back.

The parent phone call remains a suitable way to contact parents. When calling, some basic guidelines include:

1. Never call when you are angry. Calm yourself before ever calling anyone. Ask yourself whether calling is the best way to communicate the issue.
2. Script out what you will say. Create a template for your calls, and use it.
3. When possible, use the school phone. You are a professional, and professionals use office phones.
4. Keep the calls short and to the point. Always be diplomatic. Talk about the student's behavior with no opinions or general parenting advice thrown in.
5. Have a way to get off the phone quickly.
6. If you leave a message, know that the student or any family member may hear the message and/or erase it.

SCRIPT FOR PARENT PHONE CALL HOME

1. Identify yourself and know with whom you are speaking.
2. State why you are calling. Example: "I am calling because Sam has not turned in any assignments for the past two weeks. When students do not complete assignments, they are at risk of not passing and are not learning important material."
3. State a solution to the problem. Parents often do not know how to fix the problem and want to hear your solutions.
4. Get parent support for solutions.

5. Inform parents of follow-up if there will be more calls, notes, or messages.
6. Find a way to diplomatically get off the phone. "I need to let you go now because I have to make several other calls this afternoon."
7. After you have written out the script, ask yourself whether you really need to make the call at all or this is something that can be handled with the student at school.
8. Keep the script, and write in parent comments. Documentation is critical for getting further help for students, such as special education referrals or administrative support.
9. Know that although written notes of phone calls should be kept, they can also be requested/subpoenaed in serious cases. Example: A teacher was sued because a student in her class didn't learn to read. When the teacher's lawyer saw the documentation of numerous parent phone calls, requests for parent conferences, and reports of previous interventions by the teacher, the lawyer could develop a winning case for the teacher.
10. If a parent is not helpful, document the comments, and do not call again. If a parent is belligerent or rude, get off the phone and document.

Parent Conferences

Many of the guidelines for phone calls apply to parent conferences. Whether required by the school or are parent or teacher initiated, always prepare for a conference. Some guidelines include:

1. Know the school culture for conferences. Do you schedule them? Are there certain days when all parents are invited to schedule appointments?
2. If a parent contacts you requesting a meeting, schedule it when you have time for the conference at the school. Always meet in the school—never at a coffee shop or other off-campus spot. It's not professional.
3. Make sure that the family member attending is the legal guardian. Know with whom you will meet.
4. Consider having a counselor, trusted colleague, special education interventionist, or administrator sit in on the conference. In some states, union representatives are commonly invited to sit in on conferences. Do not hesitate to ask them. Before or at the very beginning of the conference, introduce the family member to the additional person you invited to the conference.

5. Have adult-sized chairs ready for a parent conference. Do not ask adults to sit in student-sized chairs.
6. Where should you sit? If you sit in your desk, the message you send is that you are in charge. You may want to convey this message.
7. If you sit side by side with the other adult(s) in the conference, you send the message that you are equals. Many good conferences are conducted with adult-sized chairs at a table.
8. Sitting at a table allows for showing student work. All participants are looking at the work together. Keep copies of student work, and have current grade averages ready to discuss with the parent.
9. Use the sandwich approach to a conference. Start with a positive statement (consider a delicious slice of bread). Next, bring out the meat of the conference. End on a positive note (the second slice of bread).
10. Parents often do not have any idea about how to help their child with academics or behavior. If behaviors have gone undisciplined for years, it is tough to teach parents how to improve their child's behavior in a short conference.
11. Address the biggest issues in the conference because not everything can be fixed at once.
12. If a follow-up conference, call, or e-mail conversation is needed, schedule it, and hand the date and time to the parent.
13. If a parent becomes belligerent, end the conference, and inform the person to speak to the administrator in the future. You do not have to put up with drunk, high, or difficult family members.
14. When a parent brings the student, the tone of the conference is completely different. Although three-way conferences have many benefits, how the conference is conducted is different.
15. If a parent brings the student's sibling, you and the parent should agree on how to have that sibling sit outside of the room and read or color during the conference. Some schools provide daycare for conferences when the whole school has conferences scheduled.

Just how far can you go to convince a parent to do what is needed to help the student achieve success? One teacher informed a parent that her child slept a lot in class and recommended an earlier bedtime. The parent said, "Well, you'll have to call me to remind me to put him to bed that early." The persistent teacher said, "Good, I like that plan." She called every school night for several weeks, and the parent finally said she would continue the earlier bedtimes. Do we commend this teacher? Did her advice solve the problem? Should a teacher take on such a responsibility? Ask six of your friends these questions. Make sure three of them are teachers, and compare the answers.

I can remember meeting a parent whose child showed every sign of becoming a pot smoker and alcoholic in the second year of high school. The parent asked me whether I had any idea of why his grades had dropped and he seemed so completely different than he had in middle school. I suggested that she talk with him about everything he does and that she monitor his friends and his activities closely. I also suggested that she schedule an appointment with the guidance counselor. That's what most teachers can do within the culture of their schools.

What about the parent who takes the child out of school for a vacation? Does that merit a conference? I teach at a private college where the annual cost for tuition, fees, and room and board is approaching $50,000 a year. One day, before class, my college student said to me, "My parents have tickets for an NFL game this week, on a school day. They want to know if it's OK if I miss class." My reply was direct, "No, it's not OK. You get a zero averaged in to your grade any day you skip class, and a large amount of information that you will miss is on the final exam." She did not go to the game. I later asked myself, and several colleagues, "What kind of parent asks their child to skip a college class when they are paying so much for it?" That student is now a teacher. I wonder how she feels when parents pull children out of her classes.

When I was a high school teacher, I remember the parents who wrote notes to excuse their children on days after rock concerts and when their teenager woke up too hungover to go to school. Of course, those excused absence notes didn't say rock concert or hangover but rather flu or cold. We all knew that the parents were lying, but the administrators at the time said that they had to believe what the parent wrote. I repeat these stories so that you see that often you can't say the truth to parents. Wouldn't you like to say "Don't let your fourteen-year-old go to a rock concert on a school night" or "Supervise your child so that he or she doesn't get drunk"? School and social norms may not permit this. You can, and should, always point out behaviors that you do see to parents and suggest that they seek further appointments with counselors.

It is acceptable to say "On six days since the first of the month, your son has put his head down on his desk and slept or tried to for at least 20 minutes of our first-period class. When I wake him, he is very groggy. He is missing valuable instruction." Next, show grades and sample work. Teachers can and should document observable behaviors. These can be shared with a parent.

Communicating with Colleagues

While visiting some schools in New Zealand, I saw huge, wall-sized calendars on whiteboards in the teachers' workroom. On these whiteboards were dates for major exams, field trips, special speakers, and other events for the whole year. Teachers were encouraged to write in as many of their activities as possible and communicate them as far in advance as possible. This idea needs to be replicated in every school on the planet.

Imagine knowing in advance when your colleagues would be taking students out of the school. Wouldn't planning be easier with a system for communication? Of course, it would.

I have worked with wonderful colleagues and toxic ones. Some lovely people let everyone know what's going on in their classrooms, whereas others shut the door and want to keep secrets. The worst communication from colleagues is when they tell your students negative stories about you. That's right. Mrs. B may tell students in her class that they shouldn't even bother being in (name of class) because the teacher just isn't very good. Ouch. Don't be a Mr. or Mrs. B.

Again, let's go back to the Golden Rule: Do unto others as you would have them do unto you. Be nice and be professional. Professionals don't gossip about other teachers or about students.

Always use professional language in school. Because I work with administrators in workshops on teacher induction, I hear stories that teachers are using words such as suck, blows, and considerably worse profanity—with students and colleagues. Unheard of even twenty years ago, this kind of communication is not acceptable.

What are some positive suggestions for improving communication among colleagues?

1. Say hello, good morning, and how are you to colleagues and wait for a response. Listen to the response.
2. When a student says something about another teacher, pass that compliment on to the teacher. If a student says something negative, ask the student not to say that in a public venue such as your classroom.
3. If the student feels there is an issue with another teacher, recommend that the student see the teacher, a counselor, or an administrator.
4. Build a network of positive people in your department or hallway. Share successes with them, and ask to hear their success stories.
5. At the end of a workday, ask colleagues to share the best thing that happened.
6. Discuss academics with colleagues. Share lesson plans and ideas. Share what works.
7. When someone is sick, send a note or card.
8. Bring in chocolate or fruit or nuts, and share them from time to time.
9. Don't wait for your administrator to make positive communications happen. Start a grassroots positive communication plan.
10. Celebrate important occasions—birthdays, babies, and the teachers' children's successes. Accentuate the positive.

And for the truly toxic moments:

1. If a teacher talks to you in a negative manner, you have options. You may state assertively, "I won't listen to such negative comments," and walk away. Some people laugh and say, "I can't believe anybody would ever say that. Good-bye."
2. If you are insulted, you should walk away and inform the administration that you are being harassed. When reporting the incident, do not embellish, but state exactly what, when, and how the teacher made the remark.
3. Unfortunately, you have to decide when to be nice, be quiet, kill someone with kindness, or report a colleague for truly unprofessional communication. Like so many questions about education, the answer is "it all depends."

COMMUNICATION WITH ADMINISTRATORS

What do you seek in a boss? Do you want someone who is supportive, caring, and well aware of your skills and talents? Do you want someone who just leaves you alone? Should your principal be someone from whom you can learn, and learn a lot? As your evaluator, should the administrator also be the one to whom you turn with your questions and issues? Should your principal be someone who helps you to problem solve? Should he or she be nice?

Now, what do you think your boss/principal expects from you? Does the principal expect you to solve every issue on your own or with the help of another teacher? Does the principal believe your mentor or department chair is the one charged with listening to your stories? Is the principal so busy that he or she has no time to talk with you about anything?

Establishing a working relationship with a principal (or any school administrator) is not something that happens automatically. Most administrators are so busy putting out the fires of student misbehaviors, parent complaints, sports events, busses, finances, and buildings, they don't have much time for building relationships with teachers. Too many administrators might say that they just want their teachers to be in their rooms and working. Ninety-nine percent of principals would probably say that they don't like surprises.

Cunningham (2009) wrote that all teachers should "Maintain a record of all communication with colleagues, administrators, students, parents, and volunteers" (p. 29). She suggests a log with a name, date, form of contact, purpose of communication, and result. Although teachers have dozens, maybe hundreds, of contacts daily with the people in the school, this may not be a feasible idea as it exists, but the concept of keeping some records is a very helpful one.

New teachers should not count on a principal reaching out to them. Additionally, a veteran teacher whose school gets a new principal can't depend on the new principal reaching out. What should a teacher communicate to the busy principal, and how should the contact be made?

1. Teachers should keep updated contact information in the principal's office. Most often done through the administrative assistant/secretary, this includes contact address, phone, and emergency contact person.
2. Even if the principal does not request it, a teacher should ensure that the classroom management plan, with its rules, consequences, and positives, is on file with the administrator in charge of student discipline (paper or electronic).
3. A copy of the first newsletter sent home to parents should also be sent to the principal. If this is an e-mail, just copy the principal.
4. Additional newsletters or syllabi that are important should be shared.
5. Principals do not like to be asked questions in the hallway that require considerable thought or research. Schedule an appointment for a big question.
6. Principals (OK, most principals) will not want to be the first person in your line of questions about school guidelines and events. Principals expect you to ask other teachers in the hallway, the teacher who is the event organizer, or a mentor teacher your questions. (Remember, principals are busy putting out big fires.)
7. Principals may not like questions during faculty meetings. They may expect you to think about options and possibilities for a time before talking about them. Few people seek open confrontation in a meeting even if they say it's always great to ask a question.
8. If you feel that you need support when talking with a principal, ask for the support according to the culture of the school. In some schools, it is quite common for a teacher to ask the union representative to sit in on a potentially difficult situation. In other schools, you can bring a teacher from down the hall to join you. Of course, bringing another person to a conference is viewed as confrontational and may break the trust level, but there are times when teachers need the support and protection of others.
9. The phrase "chain of command" is heard in a lot of schools. It refers to following protocol for incidents and communication. For example, a teacher does not pick up a phone and call a school board member about an issue at school. First, that teacher should discuss the issue with a trusted colleague, then the principal, and possibly go to the superintendent with an administrator to discuss the issue. Perhaps the

issue should be discussed with a colleague and then a union representative before even going to the administrator. That is what the chain of command is all about. Know the chain in your school and district to avoid huge conflicts.

Communication with the Administrator about Evaluations

Supervising personnel is a major part of an administrator's job. The principal is charged with having caring, competent, and effective teachers in classrooms. How should you be supervised, and what kinds of communication will help you to get positive evaluations?

1. Know the evaluation system of your school/district. This should be explained to all teachers at the beginning of each year because changes happen.
2. Clinical supervision means that the observer/evaluator will conference with you before an observation takes place. A trained supervisor will ask "What do you want me to observe for?" Ask the observer to watch how you phrase questions, how many times students get to interact with you, or the amount of on-task behaviors shown by students.
3. During the observation, a supervisor will take notes. His or her notes should be about teacher and student behaviors without judgmental commentary. Here are a couple of examples: "Teacher asked 23 questions during the 50-minute class" or "Two students did not have books open during the lesson."
4. After an observation, the teacher and supervisor should talk about the notes and the class. Teachers should be ready to answer the question "How do you think the lesson went?" because this question is a good starting point for communication about an observation. Be honest! Observers often ask "Was this a typical lesson, and was this fairly typical student behavior?"
5. The teacher should have a written copy of the notes from the observation as well as notes from the conference after the observation.
6. If a teacher disagrees with an observation, there should be a means for writing a response that is attached to the report.

The walk-through observation has become quite popular in schools because it takes only 5 to 10 minutes. With this style of observation, administrators are looking for patterns of what is going on in the classroom as they observe unannounced for a few minutes from time to time. If this is part of a teacher's evaluation, there should still be communication afterward between the observer and the teacher.

Inviting an administrator into your classroom to see a successful activity or lesson can be a very good idea. This indicates your self-confidence, and it adds to the ways that an administrator can see your work. By making the invitation truly an invitation, goodwill is promoted. Consider having the students write the invitation and maybe even deliver it if appropriate.

How else are teachers evaluated? The creation of portfolios is another way to evaluate teachers' work. Even if your school doesn't require a portfolio, you should keep samples of student work, resources that you have created, and proof of professional learning. If you get to have an end-of-year conference with your evaluator, show your portfolio, and lead the administrator to know your work. Talk about the value of workshops you attended and how you learned new skills that led to improvements in your teaching and student learning.

What about informal evaluation? Some principals ask students about their teachers but not in a formal, measurable means. They may just ask in the hallway or while students wait for a bus. Principals are often approached by parents who tell them positive comments or complaints about their children's teachers. Sometimes, principals ask other teachers down the hall about the work of a colleague.

You, as a teacher, can't control who a principal asks about your work or who talks to your principal. You can, however, keep good documentation of the work you do and keep your principal informed of your successes. I would like to tell principals that they shouldn't believe everything a parent says about a teacher, just as the teacher shouldn't believe everything a student or parent says about the principal. The same is true for what other teachers say.

Teachers should know that their evaluation begins long before the formal evaluation process starts. During orientation and back-to-school workshops, a teacher's demeanor, dress, and participation are being evaluated. Don't sit in the back row and knit during a meeting! Sit in the front, take notes, and don't text on your phone.

Every day, an evaluation is being made of your work habits. Do you arrive on time? Are you pleasant in the office? Do you get your reports in on time? Do you avoid gossip? Everything adds up for your final evaluation whether the data was gathered formally or informally.

Communication Outside of the Classroom

When I was in elementary school, there were monthly PTA meetings for parents. The parents attended a meeting, followed by coffee and cookies. Each meeting had a topic, such as the school lunch program, fundraising for equipment, or an explanation of the curriculum. My mother learned "new math" at a PTA meeting so that she could help me with math at home. Programs on reading and art were always popular. The principal ran the meetings, but teachers sometimes spoke. The teachers mingled with the families over the coffee and cookies.

Although parent open houses still exist and PTA or PTO organizations are still active in some schools, today's busy parents/family members probably don't attend with the regularity my mother did (see, for example, www.pta.org/about/ or http://pto.org/about.html for information about the national Parent Teacher Association or the Parent Teacher Organization). How much should families and the entire community know about what's going on in schools, and how can they find out about the work of schools?

Just as the chain of command was discussed with regard to communication with administrators, so too should this chain be followed when a teacher wants to publicize what's going on in the classroom. Teachers do not just type up news releases and send them to the local paper. The logistics of getting good news out to the public are complicated. What should teachers know and do about communications to the general public?

1. If your classroom has a unique project that can be showcased, work with administrators about how to present the students' work.
2. Collaborate with the art teacher for art shows in local venues, such as bank lobbies or public libraries.
3. Team with the music teacher for special song presentations. Example: The foreign language classes can sing at a school or community event. (One French teacher had her students sing Christmas carols in French on the local town square for two afternoons every winter. Of course, this can't be done in many districts, but the idea is to get the public to see what students are doing in a positive way.)
4. Families love to see their students' pictures in local newspapers. This is routine for the athletes in a school district. How could the students in a play or those in the chess club be featured in a newspaper article?
5. Always know whom to contact about school publicity for any event. Follow the guidelines regarding student privacy. Double-check the spellings of names in any communication.
6. Edit communications that go out to the public very carefully. Have at least one other teacher/administrator edit the communication as well. Misspelled words and grammatical mistakes in any communication from teachers will cause complaints and make all teachers look bad.
7. Don't overdo communications, but choose wisely what should be noteworthy news.

When families are invited to school events, careful planning must be in place. There should be a purpose for inviting families to a showcase of events. Concerts, art fairs, sports events, and science fairs take a lot of time and planning. Some additional considerations for school events include:

1. What is the purpose of the event? What is the main objective? Consider writing objectives for the event like you would write for a lesson plan. By the end of this event, the students will . . . , the parents will . . . , or the teachers will . . .
2. Are all families invited, and are families informed in writing? Are invitations in multiple languages?
3. Are times appropriate for parent participation?
4. Will snacks be served?
5. Who is in charge of each part of the event?
6. Who will clean up after the event?
7. How will the event be evaluated for continuation?
8. What were the costs of the event? Is the cost worth the value of the event?

The Teacher Is Always a School Representative

While walking through a craft fair in the town where I live, I overhead a teacher talking about her job. She said, in essence, "It's awful teaching at the school. The kids are terrible, the parents don't care, and I'm counting the days until I can get my pension. No one wants to work there anymore." I was offended because I pay that woman's salary with my taxes, and I don't even have children at the school. This was not how she should have been communicating with the public.

We all know about the negative publicity that has been generated regarding low qualifications of teachers. Many articles have grown out of the issue that teachers simply don't know their content. I heard a noted education lobbyist say that the whole firestorm surrounding unqualified teachers started when one teacher told one congressman that one teacher at her school was terribly unqualified. This may or may not be the whole story, but it has a ring of truth to it.

Every teacher represents the school at all times. Without campaigning door to door for a school tax hike, a teacher can influence the passage or failure of the referendum by conversations in the grocery store. The school's reputation is either tarnished or embellished by what teachers say. When teachers seek jobs, they often choose to not apply for positions in schools with weak reputations. Be careful with every word. Yes, teachers have the right to free speech, but with freedom comes responsibility.

KEYS FOR SUCCESS

1. Successful teachers monitor their words to students, parents, colleagues, and administrators.

2. Successful teachers find better ways to communicate than with sarcasm.
3. Successful teachers take responsibility for learning how to communicate with their administrators.
4. Successful teachers keep parents/families informed of the successes in their classrooms, always mindful of the privacy of individual students.
5. Successful teachers work with others in their schools and districts to promote positive communications to the communities they serve.
6. Successful teachers don't gossip in public about the school's problems.

Chapter Ten

Manage Time and Stress

> Successful teachers are intentional about time and stress management.
>
> You feel your heartbeat race and your adrenaline rise as if you were ready for a marathon, but instead of running, you are standing at the door of your classroom, ready to greet students. Excitement and stress are a bit alike and actually help you to be an enthusiastic teacher, but too much stress wears you down and may lead to burnout. Knowing that the demands of teaching and life do cause tension, what can you do to keep stress at a manageable level, enabling you to be an effective teacher throughout your career? (Clement, 2017b)

Ask any practicing teacher about time, and they will probably say "There's never enough of it." Ask them about stress, and they will say "There's too much of it." Lack of time and stress lead to burnout, and leaving the teaching profession contributes to the teacher shortage. Additionally, teachers who burn out and leave teaching may have difficulty finding another job with the regular pay, health care, retirement, and vacation time of teaching. So what are the answers?

TIME MANAGEMENT

Everyone has probably heard the age-old adages about time management.

1. Just say no. Overcommitting leaves you feeling like you have no time for anything. This is true for school and home.
2. Make to-do lists, follow them, and cross things off.
3. Get up early or stay up late, but do not do both.
4. Make routines and follow them.
5. Get your students to do some of your work for you.

6. Go in to the school early or stay late, but don't do both.
7. Use technology to do some of the drudgery work, like grade averaging.
8. Plan ahead—way ahead.
9. Ask family members to do their part.
10. Get rid of clutter so that you don't waste time hunting things.
11. Accept that there are only 24 hours in a day.
12. Keep on top of paperwork. You have to meet deadlines for reports, testing, and grading.

As valuable as some of these bits of folk wisdom are, what are some other strategies to manage time at work and at home?

Time Management at Work

The pressures put on teachers are real, and honestly, there is never enough time. However, do you know where and how you spend your time at work? Before you can control some of your time, you need to know where that time is spent. Here are two activities.

Write out a blank day-by-day chart for a typical school week.

Monday:
7
8
9
10
11
12
1
2
3

Repeat for Tuesday through Friday. Now, for each hour at work, write what you do. No cheating—you have to write what you really do. After one week, look at your hour-by-hour list. Can any changes be made? Can any blocks of time be carved out for paper grading? Lesson planning?

The next step is to talk about how you spend your school day with a trusted colleague. Ask whether they see any possible areas for change. You must really push yourself to listen to the colleague and to strive to make those changes suggested.

Can you, within the culture of the school, do some thinking outside of the box with regard to school time? In one high school, the English department saw a way to develop more planning and grading time. On Fridays, their students always took a vocabulary test and then had reading time. On Fridays, the English teachers then had time to plan for the next week and to grade papers.

Although it could be argued that these teachers were losing 20 percent of their instructional time (one day out of five), it could also be argued that students were still meeting the state standards for vocabulary and reading. Having students read on Fridays seemed a better solution than having students read whole books aloud in class time, which some middle and high school teachers have implemented because students don't read much at home. I am not necessarily advocating this but suggesting that teachers should brainstorm ideas.

Some teachers have students grade each other's papers to save time. In reality, teachers must do the grading and the grade recording to comply with FERPA (Family Educational Rights and Privacy Act) (see www2.ed.gov/policy/gen/guid/fpco/ferpa/students.html). Students can correct their own papers while teachers give visual and verbal feedback. Students can peer-edit and check each other's work without applying a grade. Teachers can decide when to collect and grade papers. Students who complete online quizzes can get instant feedback and good practice with interactive drills.

By keeping detailed lesson plans, time is saved the next time a lesson is taught. For classes, teachers generally write shortened plans, but by keeping a notebook for each subject with detailed plans, the second time around is so much easier. With technology, PowerPoints and other applications give teachers the chance to prepare material once and use it over and over. Trust me, I have recycled many lessons.

Does collaborating with other teachers save or eat up time? It all depends on your colleagues and their work styles. You may have to avoid some colleagues who will eat up your time with their complaints and negativity. Alternately, sometimes, collaboration will save hours of time. Decide ahead of time and plan accordingly.

Are meetings time wasters? A good meeting is a productive one. Although you will see colleagues grading papers, texting, or playing games on the phones during meetings, the truth is that when everyone pays attention, a meeting takes less time. Sometimes, you do just have to endure a meeting, but paying attention is noticed by your bosses. When you run a meeting, have an agenda and stick to it. Try the stand-up meeting, where you tell everyone that the meeting will be very short if everyone stands up during the meeting and focuses.

At-Home and Personal Time Management

Remember the hour-by-hour chart you made of your school day for a week? The first step for personal time management is to do the same thing for all seven days of the week and to complete it honestly for a typical week, or try the circle of time activity. Draw a big circle to represent 24 hours of your day. Yes, everybody does get 24 hours in a day! Now, make the big circle into a pie chart. For the first pie chart, mark the pieces of the pie for a workday. Example:

- Time spent sleeping
- Time spent commuting
- Time spent in school
- Time spent outside of school on work
- Time spent cooking, cleaning, or with children
- Time spent in personal activities, such as watching TV or reading
- Time spent exercising

You should make two more pie charts—one for Saturday and one for Sunday. Again, you have to be honest with how you really spend your days, or this time management activity doesn't help you. For the Saturday and Sunday charts, remember the following:

- Time spent running errands
- Time spent cleaning the house and doing the laundry
- Time spent going out to eat
- Time spent with entertainment—movies, TV, on the phone with friends
- Time spent with children's activities
- Time spent dating or with spouse
- Time spent in church or community activities

With three circle pie charts in front of you, decide whether this is how you really want to spend your time. Make new circles with your preferred time for a workday and for Saturday and Sunday. Now, the toughest part of this time management fix is to change your schedule so that your real-time circle looks more like your preferred-time circle. How have some educators done this?

    An acquaintance of mine teaches in Beijing, where traffic is horrendous. His commute was growing from 45 minutes one way to sometimes an hour and 45 minutes each way in stressful traffic. He and his wife came to a tough decision. They moved from a house they rented to an apartment, and he now has a 15-minute walk to work. That was a dramatic change and one that took a lot of planning and time to implement, but the result was more than worth the bother of moving.

    Sometimes, guilt keeps us from changing time-consuming habits. I was raised that I should cook meals at home to save money and to feed my family. Cooking, and doing it well, is time consuming. I have discovered that buying prepared dishes from our nearby grocery store deli is not only a time saver but also still provides us with cooked vegetables. Everyone has to decide on changes like this one. Enlisting your family to do some of the cooking, laundry, and household chores not only saves you time but builds responsibility in the other family members.

Years ago, student-teaching supervisors, and even principals, admonished new teachers to not get married or have a baby until they were established as teachers. Of course, these are highly personal decisions, and only the teacher can make these choices. However, there are only so many hours in a day and only so many days in a week.

I am often asked how I have had time for a career in teaching, a career in writing, and traveling around the world to over forty-five countries. My answer is that my husband and I chose not to have children and my husband is incredibly supportive about all of my work. I do not state this as a solution for everyone, but I do encourage others to think deeply about whether, when, and whom they marry and their decisions about whether they have children and how many they have. Our big decisions affect our little decisions tremendously. I know dozens of people who say that they wish that they had started their families later or that they had not caved in to family pressure to have children. These are tough, personal decisions with lifelong effects on how you will spend your time.

For some people, having children is the biggest joy of their lives, and the children keep them centered and happy. That's the funny thing about time and stress management—what might be the biggest stressor for some may be the best thing for others.

STRESS MANAGEMENT

You don't have to write a doctoral dissertation on the pressures of teaching to see what causes stress for teachers. The list is long. There is the accountability movement that imposes responsibility on teachers for high student achievement and increasingly higher test scores. The stress of dealing with large numbers of unprepared students in all grade levels is a constant. Striving to maintain positive classroom management when more and more students enter our classrooms with emotional and behavioral issues is a genuine challenge.

Teachers talk about dealing with more and more unloved and uncared-for students in their classes. Although there are issues of working with children living in high-poverty homes, the increase of children who don't have caring parents or adults in their lives crosses all socioeconomic lines.

I tried to explain to a teacher in China that schools in the United States provide breakfast to children because their parents don't feed them in the morning, and she was convinced that she misunderstood my English because surely there were not parents who didn't give their children breakfast. I didn't even go on to explain that many schools provide backpacks of food for children on Fridays to ensure that they have something to eat over the weekends. She would have certainly thought I was making that up. How many schools have clothing closets to help students get something clean and warm to wear? Many, many schools do this, and some teachers spend their own money to stock those closets.

Dealing with parents and families causes stress for teachers, as does working with difficult administrators and colleagues. Today's teachers feel beleaguered by negative public attitudes toward the education system. Herman and Reinke (2015) have written that there is an "assault on teachers" caused by the many challenges they face today. "Teachers may project their stress onto their students, making it more likely that students will experience stress themselves, and thereby less likely they will be open to learning" (p. 4).

Basically, today's teachers are asked to do more with less. They are asked to raise other people's children and to be the nurse, the psychologist, and the adult role model for students, all while teaching academics. The expectations are high, and the stressors are real.

Stress Management in General

Several years ago, I attended an all-day stress-reduction seminar taught by a professional in the field, according to the brochure. The instructor took all day to explain the three big steps of stress management:

1. You must identify your stressors.
2. You must identify what can be done about your stressors.
3. You must do what you identified in step 2.

One of the workshop examples was the stress one woman felt about cooking Thanksgiving dinner for a large extended family and in-laws every year. She had come to hate that week in November, and the stress was making her sick every season. The instructor said, "Why do you have to cook for everyone? What is another feasible solution? What would it take for you not to have stress about this meal and holiday?" The woman with the stress said that she wished someone else would simply volunteer to host the event or that they would use a community room and have a potluck. "So," replied the instructor, "do it." "No one ever volunteers, and the older family members might feel slighted if we moved to a community room," said the woman. She continued, "I just feel that I should do it." The instructor replied, "Stop that *now*, and tell your family you can't host Thanksgiving. They will have to figure something out." That's how you solve stress.

Did you see the three steps from the Thanksgiving example? The stressor was identified, a stress breaker was identified, and all that was left was for the woman to put the solution into action. Step three is the hardest part. By the way, I was not that woman, but my husband and I created a wonderful low-stress Thanksgiving tradition. We eat alone that day—just the two of us with a little turkey-for-two meal that is super easy to make. We have turned down a lot of offers, including ones from relatives, but we keep this wonderful day to ourselves. It works so well. A lot of people tell me that they are jealous of our tradition and wish that they could do it. I smile and say, "What's stopping you?" The world doesn't stop turning when we destress by making positive decisions.

The next time you are in line at the supermarket, skim over the front page of the magazines while you wait. I am sure that at least one of the magazines will have an article about stress management. I feel like I have read them all and that they often say the same things. The common stress relief approaches include:

1. Sleep eight hours a night.
2. Eat a balanced, healthy diet.
3. Exercise daily.
4. Don't overbook yourself with too many volunteer duties.
5. Find what gives you joy, and build time for that activity.
6. Schedule downtime and vacation time.
7. Give up perfectionism.
8. Limit caffeine and alcohol.
9. If the stress is overwhelming, seek medical advice. There may be an underlying physical issue for stress.
10. Have a network of trusted family members and friends.
11. Stay away from toxic people.
12. Find a purpose in life, and seek strength from religion.
13. Get a new hobby.
14. Try meditation, yoga, or prayer.
15. Go somewhere fun but not too expensive (the mall, the park, a movie).
16. Get out into nature and walk.
17. Sit quietly in a happy space.
18. Make a room of your house a haven.
19. Listen to favorite music.
20. Read for fun.

How do you know whether you are stressed? Herman and Reinke (2015) made a list that includes:

- I feel tension in my shoulders.
- I get restless and fidgety.
- I can't think clearly.
- I can't focus.
- I feel anxious.
- I feel tired and worn out.
- I feel overwhelmed.
- I feel tense.
- I feel irritable. (p. 12)

Although these are natural reactions to a tough day, as a teacher you don't want to feel this way all day and every day. Long-term feelings of stress can lead to real illnesses.

Dealing with Specific School Stressors

A huge school stressor is the "decision that came from the top." The decision could be about anything—a new reading program, a new teacher evaluation format, a change of schedule for classes, or making teachers change rooms. Change causes stress for almost everyone. Communication helps with change. Don't immediately jump to the thought that "this is the end of the world." Ask questions about timelines, and discuss changes with a mentor, colleagues, and the administrator. Remember to talk sensibly to yourself too. Remind yourself that you can do this and some changes are good things.

I worked in one school setting where the administrator made announcements about big changes that actually never happened. That was extremely frustrating. As a faculty, we eventually learned to wait to hear final decisions and not to start on any new project until it became official. If your school leaders talk about changes that don't happen, practice patience. Ask about timelines and implementation start dates. If they don't have dates yet, know that they may not.

Teaching has long been considered a very isolating job. Surrounded by students all day, you can still be lonely and in need of adult conversation. It is not good to shut your door and never talk with those down the hall. Stopping for coffee (try decaf) during the planning period or eating your sandwich with good colleagues can make a difference in how you get through the day.

If you can't find colleagues across the hall, consider online networks. Kappa Delta Pi is an honor society for teachers, and its website, www.kdp.org/, has an online social media site for members. It's like Facebook, but it is password protected and for members only, and the discussions are monitored to ensure that professionalism is maintained. Other professional associations have question-and-answer sites online. Some teachers join specific blogs to talk about their teaching. Be careful about what you post on any site because this information can go viral. You might also look at teachers-teachers.com, Teacher2Teacher, or schoolspring.com on Facebook for interesting posts.

The last time I went to Teacher2Teacher, I saw this wonderful quote from a teacher named William Anderson: "There's nothing more powerful than having people to lean on and celebrate with in this tough work we do." Quotes such as this do a lot to help us all get through the week.

Professional learning communities (PLCs) offer grassroots professional development for teachers and are directed by teachers. A PLC can tackle a big question with some action research, or read a book together, or look at test results at the end of the year. PLCs not only help teachers to understand and solve issues but also provide the opportunity for ownership of school policies, leadership, and collegiality. If you are reading this book alone, start a reading group or PLC to read together. And, yes, it's OK to have coffee, cookies, and chocolate at these meetings.

Because so much of stress management is dependent upon isolating the stressors and deciding what to do about them, consider PLCs to talk about the really tough issues. A group of teachers can discuss their successes with students with behavioral issues or students on the autism spectrum. They can request the professional development speakers that the district brings in for workshops or make suggestions for how to better manage early dismissal days. There is strength in numbers, and having a group formulate a request and support their request with data may make a big difference in how the administrator perceives the request.

Another way to use data to get what we need in schools is to do our homework. I am always amazed when a teacher says that he or she doesn't read any professional literature because there is nothing in the field that relates to his or her work. There are professional journals, teacher magazines, and literally millions of books about teaching issues. Find them, read them, and discuss them to lower your stress by problem solving.

Doing our homework is another way to lower stress. I know that there are evenings and weekends that you don't want to use for work, but sometimes, a bit of work at home puts you ahead of the game and makes you feel ready and less stressed. A former colleague of mine had a very small bag for her teaching work. She looked around her room at the end of the day and asked herself, "Is there anything that I really should take home to do?" If her answer was yes, then she put only the amount of work that she could do in one hour in her bag. That's why the bag was small!

I have known other teachers who limit their evening and weekend work by timing it and having some free evenings. Their examples included working two hours on Sunday and then one hour on Monday, Tuesday, and Thursday. They knew that they never had to work at home on Wednesdays, Fridays, or Saturdays. Another very organized teacher said that she did her work on Saturday morning, with time for lots of coffee, and then felt very free the rest of the weekend. I teach at the college level and still find that a few hours of extra preparation on Sunday make the week run smoothly. I guard my late Friday afternoons and Saturdays fiercely.

Another Self-Evaluation

Just as you made the lists of how you spend your daily hours and the circle pie charts to see where the time really goes, consider a list of stressors and your reaction to each one. For each of the following school issues, rate the issue on a scale of 0 to 5, where 0 indicates no stress and 5 indicates a big stressor.

ISOLATING SCHOOL STRESSORS

1. My administrator does not know what I really do.
2. My administrator does not support my work.
3. I need more supplies for teaching.
4. I need professional development on certain topics (make a list).
5. Student behavior is a real issue/problem with this year's classes.
6. Working with English language learners has become a real issue/problem.
7. Working with the special needs students has become a real issue/problem.
8. Working with colleagues in special needs/special education causes more stress than help.
9. Working with teachers in my grade/subject level causes more stress than support.
10. I need to have more blocks of time to teach and fewer interruptions.
11. I need more preparation time in the school day.
12. I need more secretarial/administrative assistant help.
13. The demands of how we use technology are stressful.
14. More updated computers are needed.
15. Working with parents is stressful for me.
16. Standardized testing is stressful.
17. Being given the curriculum with strict guidelines is stressful.
18. Seeing other teachers not do their jobs causes stress.
19. Seeing students not get their needed help is stressful.
20. The waste of time in our school is stressful.
21. Unproductive meetings are stressful.
22. My classroom is uncomfortable—too hot, too cold, too small.
23. The never-ending needs of low-socioeconomic students causes my stress.

24. The fact that I do great work and am seldom or never recognized or thanked is stressful.
25. My colleagues are so negative.
26. Being held accountable for student progress that is out of my control is stressful.
27. Being held accountable for student behavior when the student needs a psychologist or special intervention is stressful.
28. Hearing community members say that teaching is easy or that we aren't doing our jobs is stressful.
29. Completing paperwork and grade reports is stressful.
30. Doing the job that my administrator or a secretary/administrative assistant can and should do is stressful.

Look at your responses that received a 5. List the five biggest stressors from the ones that received a five. If you didn't give a five to at least five issues, you are lucky. You may then look at the ones that received a 4 on your list. The point is that all the things can't be resolved at once. This is triage, like in an emergency room. A teacher can look at a smaller list and then make some decisions.

For the items on your short list of five issues, what can you do about them? Can you do some research, read a book, or go to a conference for new ideas? Can you enlist the support of other teachers? Are there some issues that you simply cannot control? Reinhold Niebuhr is credited with the commonly cited Serenity Prayer:

> God grant me the serenity to accept the things I cannot change; courage to change the things I can; and wisdom to know the difference. (www.beliefnet.com/prayers/protestant/addiction/serenity-prayer.aspx)

To thrive in teaching, teachers must decide what they can and cannot change. How much stress can you accept in your position? How much can you cope with before you need to change grade levels? Change schools? Change districts? Change professions? Become the boss?

Herman and Reinke (2015) discussed creating a positive cycle to combat stress. Their cycle begins by catching your negative thoughts and doing something positive. Next, continue the positivity by congratulating yourself, having a good conversation with someone else, and striving to be grateful. Laugh and continue the positivity (p. 34). I once heard a speaker say that teachers need to "talk sense to themselves." This is especially important if someone around you is talking very negatively.

Awareness of our stressors is a starting point for lowering stress. Adapting positive behaviors is a good next step. Admitting that many things are out of our control is important. Striving to see the positive helps us get through a day and a week. Building a network of mentors, friends, and positive people will always make us feel better.

What's the bottom line on stress management? Stress management is different for everyone. Gardening may be the solution for many people as a coping mechanism that lowers their stress, but gardening would raise my stress greatly! Visiting my mother lowers my stress and always puts my life back into perspective, but again, this might raise the stress for others. We each have to find our way to accept the issues in this career we have chosen and to decide how to cope with the problems and make changes for improvement.

KEYS FOR SUCCESS

1. Successful teachers know that there is only so much time in a day, and they prioritize and budget that time.
2. Successful teachers know that they can't do everything by themselves. They get help from family and friends. They work with other teachers for support.
3. Successful teachers recognize that teaching is stressful, but they identify their stressors and consider possible changes.
4. Successful teachers know that the tried-and-true adages for stress management can work.
5. Successful teachers do know when to say no.
6. Successful teachers know that they don't have to be perfect to teach and have a personal life.
7. Successful teachers know that managing stress involves many individual decisions. Stress busters for some people are causes of stress for others. Teachers have to decide what causes and lowers their stress.
8. Successful teachers know when it is time to change grade levels or schools or become an administrator.

Chapter Eleven

Grow as Professionals

> Successful teachers consider themselves professionals, working in the profession that makes all others possible.

Many teachers resent the general public's attitude toward teachers. As a teacher and teacher educator, I have encountered two very interesting conversations with strangers about this profession. Both occurred on airplanes.

I was seated next to a woman who asked why I was flying. I reported that I was a teacher educator and was going to a conference to give a presentation. She replied that she never knew that teachers had to be taught how to teach. Her words were "I just presumed teachers had a degree in something and got jobs in schools. I mean if you can read, you can teach reading, right?" Imagine her surprise when I talked about the challenging teacher education curriculum and mandated certification tests for teachers. Yes, I informed her, there was a knowledge base for teaching, and it must be learned. People don't just get college degrees and walk in off the streets to teach.

The second conversation cut me deeply to the core. On another flight, a woman asked the purpose of my flight. I informed her that I was the current president of Kappa Delta Pi, the international honor society for teachers. I was going to a college campus to speak to the students in the organization. She replied, "That's odd. I wouldn't have thought that honor students in a college would be the ones becoming teachers." Ouch. That comment hurt, but it motivated me to do even more work to honor teacher education students and practicing teachers.

WHAT DOES IT MEAN TO BE A PROFESSIONAL?

A profession is more than a job. To be a professional, the future employee must learn the knowledge base of the field, have specialized training, and complete a licensure program. Professionals are subject to the monitoring of their profession throughout their careers. Teaching meets these criteria because teachers have specialized training, the licensure process includes multiple steps in most states (costing up to $600 in some), and each state has its own system to govern entrance into and exit from teaching. Why then do many people consider teachers to be glorified babysitters or public servants rather than professionals?

There is a very old joke that a mother went to a parent/teacher conference and listened to a teacher explain what she could do to help her child achieve more in school. The parent disregarded all advice given. The parent later took her child to the doctor and did everything the doctor said to help her child. It is really not a funny joke at all but does indicate how some parents view the teaching profession.

Some people think that they know everything about teaching because they spent thirteen years in school themselves. They had good and bad teachers and they know the difference. They may quote the latest news story about a teacher fired for unprofessional behavior. Yes, there are weak apples in every barrel, including the profession of teaching, but the professionalism of teaching has increased astronomically over the years. As a teacher, what can you do to grow as a professional in your field? Where will you get help throughout your career? Do you want to become a leader in your school and perhaps become an administrator?

MENTORING AND BEING MENTORED

Even if you graduated from an outstanding teacher education program, the first few years of teaching or the first few years in a different school system can be extremely challenging. Induction programs are designed to help new hires become successful in their jobs. An induction program consists of orientation for new hires, ongoing professional development seminars throughout the year, and mentoring. Mentoring, which pairs a more experienced teacher with the new hire, can increase the retention of the new hire, raise student achievement, and perhaps most importantly, lower the stress and frustration of the new hire (see, for example, Clement, 2011).

As the teacher being mentored, how can you get the most out of being paired with another teacher? Communication can be the key. When you first meet your mentor, find out the parameters/guidelines of the program. Good questions to ask include:

1. Tell me about your first years in this school/district and your teaching career.
2. Are there specific times that we will meet?
3. Will there be an opportunity for me to observe your classes?
4. Will there be an opportunity for you to observe my classes?
5. Are you evaluating me in any way or turning in any type of report to my principal?
6. What types of questions may I ask?
7. Can we attend a workshop or conference together?
8. What have you found to be the biggest challenges with the students in our school? Why?
9. What are your three top pieces of advice for me as I start teaching here?
10. Are you available to help me organize my classroom before the first day of classes?
11. Please explain the teacher evaluation system to me, and give me your advice about getting positive evaluations.

A good mentor is a role model, a guide, and a sounding board for your ideas. Your mentor can listen to your teaching plans, providing suggestions and input before you teach lessons. A good mentor is not only a good teacher but also a good teacher educator, knowing how to gently guide a new teacher to success.

Do not feel insulted by being assigned a mentor, even though you are fully licensed teacher. Everybody needs help and support with the job of teaching. I repeat the line I have often said, "Teaching is too difficult a job to do alone and too important a job to do alone." When teachers work to support each other, the chances for success are greatly enhanced. Allow yourself to be mentored throughout your career and then to mentor others.

Once you have a few years of experience, consider becoming a mentor. In many districts, the call for mentors is made early in the spring semester, and mentor training is offered to prepare mentors for their roles. In mentor training, teachers learn about the tenets of adult learning because mentoring a new teacher requires different skills than teaching K–12 students. Just as pedagogy means the study of teaching children, andragogy is the study of teaching adults. Mentoring involves learning a new set of teaching skills.

Being a mentor can be a wonderful experience. Some mentors find that they really enjoy this form of professional development and decide to pursue a career in it. Mentoring new teachers can be a stepping-stone toward getting an administrative position because hiring and inducting new employees is a big part of administrators' jobs. Most mentors feel greatly rewarded by giving back to the profession by mentoring a beginning teacher. If administration isn't for you, mentoring is a way to stay in the role of classroom teacher yet grow as a professional.

THE SUPPORT OF A PROFESSIONAL ASSOCIATION

For two years, I served as the president of Kappa Delta Pi (KDP), the international honor society for educators (www.kdp.org). As I gave talks around the United States about the value of joining this professional association, I realized that most new members who were college students were joining just for a line on their résumés, yet Kappa Delta Pi is a professional association that supports teachers throughout their careers, from the sophomore year of college to retirement. KDP provides online resources, traditional publications, an annual conference, local chapter activities on college campuses, and grants and scholarships. Who wouldn't join a support group this strong for less than $50 a year?

In my work with student teachers, I suggest that they join at least two professional organizations in addition to the association/union of their school district. One organization should be a general one for all teachers, such as Kappa Delta Pi, and one should be the association for their content area. Content area associations include:

1. National Association for the Education of Young Children (www.naeyc.org)
2. International Literacy Association (www.literacyworldwide.org). This is for all elementary and middle school teachers who teach language arts.
3. Association for Middle Level Education (www.amle.org)
4. National Association for Teachers of Mathematics (www.nctm.org)
5. National Association for Teachers of English (www2.ncte.org)
6. National Science Teachers Association (www.nsta.org)
7. National Council for the Social Studies (www.socialstudies.org)
8. Council for Exceptional Children (www.cec.sped.org)
9. American Council on the Teaching of Foreign Languages (www.actfl.org)
10. Music Teachers National Association (www.mtna.org)

There is literally an organization for every field of teaching as well as other specialized organizations that support teachers. I enjoy being a member of Delta Kappa Gamma, a society of "leading women educators" (www.dkg.org). This organization has maintained its small chapter organization model, and local meetings take place monthly in my town. The members raise money for scholarships for young women entering the teaching profession and donate dictionaries to all third-graders in two local school districts.

Two other general associations include Phi Delta Kappa (pdkintl.org) and the Association for Supervision and Curriculum Development (www.ascd.org). These two associations are most noted for their publications. PDK publishes the *Kappan*, and ASCD publishes *Educational Leadership*; both are worthy reads.

Why should teachers spend their own money to join and maintain their memberships in professional associations? These associations provide current information about the profession and each field of study. Teachers need to stay current about trends and issues. Would you want to see a doctor who hadn't read a medical journal since graduation from medical school? Absolutely not. Just as the knowledge base of medical research has grown, so too has the knowledge base of teaching. Your professional development will not be completed by just attending some local workshops. As a professional, you need to take charge of your growth, and being an active member of professional organizations is a proven way to do so.

Now, about joining your local teachers' association/union. The National Education Association (www.nea.org) and the American Federation of Teachers (www.aft.org) offer many advantages to their members. A district generally has a local chapter of one or the other to represent its teachers in salary negotiations and to protect members' rights. Professional development opportunities are offered, and there are many online resources. The advantages to membership include the fact that there are local, state, and national organizations for supportive services to members.

PROFESSIONAL LEARNING COMMUNITIES

The old standard for teachers' learning was the one-shot workshop. A professional developer was hired to teach a half-day workshop, and all the teachers were herded into a cafeteria or media center to learn the newest fad or technique. The speaker was paid, and some teachers learned a few new techniques or gained some insight into a new trend. I have attended dozens of these and taught many of them. Teachers can gain ideas and get inspired by a dynamic speaker, and bringing in outside experts can be a good thing. However, using the expertise of teachers themselves has gained acceptance for strong in-house professional development.

A professional development community (PLC) is one example of teacher collaboration for teacher learning and growth. A PLC was defined by Dufour, Dufour, Eaker, and Many (2006) as "an ongoing process in which educators work collaboratively in recurring cycles of collective inquiry and action research to achieve better results for the students they serve (para. 4). What does that really look like in a school?

A PLC is more than a book study group, although a book study group can be an effective way to initiate a PLC. (Have a group of teachers read this book together to discuss and critique it.) A PLC begins with a group of teachers and their administrators committing to the idea that the group members can decide what needs to be studied and how to go about studying or researching the topic. Additionally, the members need to decide how their progress and results will be assessed.

PLCs shouldn't be just another layer of work for teachers. They should replace most of the workshops and seminars that have been delivered to the teachers in the past. Adding PLCs to an already overloaded schedule of professional development will not achieve as much success as building teacher growth around the PLCs. Additional benefits from PLCs can include increased collegiality among a school's teachers, improved appreciation for and involvement with action research in the classroom, and improved instructional practice.

Some examples for teacher study might include:

1. All teachers of a grade level look at standardized test scores to identify areas that need more time for instruction.
2. A group of teachers work together to discuss implementation of a district-mandated reading or math program.
3. High school teachers from across the district meet regularly to plan for the implementation of or updating of Advanced Placement (AP) courses.
4. Middle school teachers decide to do a self-study of how reading is implemented across the curriculum in their school.
5. Small groups of teachers meet monthly to read and discuss research articles from peer-reviewed journals in their respective fields. Discussion begins on the writing of an article by the teachers about one of their best practices.
6. Teachers study the data on in-school and out-of-school student suspensions for their school. They present their findings to the entire faculty and lead a discussion of improved classroom management policies.
7. Teachers study a parent involvement program at a neighboring school and lead a discussion on a similar program at their school.

What are some challenges to the idea of grassroots teacher professional development and professional learning communities? There must be time for these communities to meet. One author, Spencer (2016), wrote that PLCs should ideally meet once a week. Although this might be extremely rare, ongoing, regularly scheduled meetings are a necessity for success. Administrators must support the PLCs and provide some initial training for the teachers who will lead the groups. There has to be accountability for the outcomes of the community's work. Some resources are needed—books, articles, and refreshments may be needed as well as additional time for teachers to conduct research.

Even if a school doesn't implement PLCs exactly as the writers and theorists describe, having teachers share their expertise with others is an important factor for in-house professional development. A teacher who attends a national conference can report about the sessions attended. Short-term book or article groups can be quite helpful for teachers to stay up to date on current issues. Just having the opportunity to talk about best practices once a month with colleagues can be very supportive for teachers.

BECOMING A TEACHER LEADER

Much has been written about teacher leadership. Coggins and McGovern (2014) wrote that implementation of teacher leadership in a school can have five important goals:

1. Improve student outcomes
2. Improve the access of high-need students to effective teachers
3. Extend the careers of teachers looking for growth opportunities
4. Expand the influence of effective teachers on their peers
5. Ensure a role for teachers as leaders in policy decisions affecting their practice (p. 16)

Berry (2014) made a call for *teacherpreneurs*, teachers who are entrepreneurs and leaders within their schools. He wrote:

> The problems of public education aren't that America's classrooms are filled with too many bad teachers or too few smart ones. Instead, policy makers are paying too little attention to mobilizing the many experts teaching today who could lead in powerful ways. (p. 8)

On a personal note, I never really wanted to leave my high school teaching career, but after eight years, I felt I didn't have any place to grow. I opted to get my doctorate and work in higher education. What if people like me had more growth opportunities within our districts? What if I could have become the lead mentor teacher for the district, for half a day, teaching in the classroom half-time? Could I have moved successfully into human resources/personnel management?

I absolutely love teaching workshops as a consultant and could have easily become the in-house professional developer for my district, yet it was a district that did not support its teachers to even attend national conferences. I recommend that all districts consider the wonderful talent within their own faculties and grow talented teachers into leaders in the schools.

What does a teacher leader do? How does one become one? Most teacher leaders are strong teachers themselves, achieving success with their students. They may enter leadership as a supervisor of a practicum student or student teacher from a nearby university. They may start sharing their best teaching ideas with colleagues or join a school committee. Emerging teacher leaders see issues that need addressing. They begin to research those issues and share their findings. Some teachers assume leadership duties in their professional associations or unions.

Many teachers feel powerless in their jobs. They feel that decisions are made at the top and filter down to them. The truth is that principals have so many roles and responsibilities that they need to share leadership duties to survive in their own jobs. Teachers can provide that leadership to their peers. "There is a solid base of individual teachers who crave leadership opportunities" (Berry, 2014, p. 11).

What are some practical examples of teacher leadership?

1. Join a committee on book selection, classroom management, test data review, or any other topic.
2. When you see an issue that needs study, start a committee to discuss the issue. Strive to find practical answers to questions that other teachers in your grade/subject area have.
3. Go to a conference, and bring your learning back to your colleagues.
4. Lead a professional learning community or book study.
5. Lead a group of teachers to observe in others' classrooms or in a neighboring school.
6. Accept a student teacher, and start a support group for others who work with student teachers because mentoring student teachers can be stressful.
7. Mentor a new teacher.
8. Volunteer to teach part of new-teacher orientation.
9. Organize a new-teacher workshop or support group that is ongoing throughout the year.
10. Develop an assessment of the value of your work in any of the above categories. Speak with your principal about the value of teacher leadership.

Many readers of this chapter will skim these ideas and say, "When is there time to do any of this? We already have to do more with less. Test preparation, dealing with underprepared students, and mounds of paperwork have today's teachers covered up. There is no time left to lead, and besides, why should I do the principal's job for no extra pay?" These are all valid statements felt by teachers throughout the country, yet there can be rewards for assuming leadership roles as a teacher.

The rewards for teacher leaders are generally intrinsic. Teachers can feel empowered by working for positive changes. Strong administrators should recognize the value of these teachers, and verbal recognition is important for any employee. The leadership role may be what is needed to keep the teacher in the profession or to lead to another role within the school or district. Becoming a leader within the school may be part of the overall career path of an educator.

THE STAGES OF A TEACHER'S CAREER

In their book, *Life Cycle of the Career Teacher*, Steffy, Wolfe, Pasch, and Enz (2000) defined the stages of teaching as novice, apprentice, professional, expert, distinguished, and emeritus. For each career stage, they suggested professional development strategies to support a teacher during those years. For example, a new teacher needs support from a mentor and an ongoing induction program, whereas a veteran teacher may seek National Board Certification as a means to grow professionally.

In his presentations, noted educator Harry Wong says that there are four steps in a teacher's career: fantasy, survival, mastery, and impact. New hires are thrilled to have a classroom, and they think that the students will all behave beautifully and brilliantly when treated as friends. This may last until Halloween, or maybe not even that long. Next, the new teacher teaches for survival—getting to the end of the day and the end of the year. With administrative support, experience, and appropriate professional development, teachers can reach the mastery level. Strong teachers leave an effect on students and affect the school as leaders (see Wong & Wong, 2009).

I call the first few weeks, and maybe months, of a teacher's career the honeymoon phase because everything looks rosy in a new job. It is good to be optimistic and positive about the school year and the students' abilities. A little naiveté is also a good thing. There are moments in any job where we just "get by," and it's OK not to make every single lesson a beautiful, creative work of art. When we gain experience, we start questioning things in our classrooms and schools. This too is a good thing.

We should question our instructional practice. Is it working for all students? Are there changes in students' needs in our classroom and school? In the college where I teach, students complete a course evaluation of my classes every semester. I am starting to see a trend that they don't have the reading level for the textbooks I have chosen and I have to find ones with easier readings. (Yes, this scares me a lot!) Additionally, more students seem to be questioning why I encourage taking notes and don't just give them the notes online. I need to be more explicit about the value of taking notes versus being given notes, and I do need to incorporate more pictures into my notes on the screen. We should all be listening to our students' feedback, but there is also a time to hold fast to certain proven instructional practices. We are, after all, the ones trained in pedagogy.

Career stages of teachers also relate to burnout and dropping out of the profession. Administrators need to know that some veteran teachers want to feel empowered. They want to have a voice and to contribute to the overall running of the school. They want to go to conferences and share what they learn. They want their expertise recognized. If these needs are not met, some teachers may seek other jobs where their expertise is recognized, such as teaching at a community college.

I once heard a retired principal talk about his self-proclaimed success as an administrator. He said that he never allowed a teacher to teach the same grade level in his elementary school for more than three years. He claimed (erroneously) that this kept their teaching fresh and kept them creating new lesson plans and materials. He did not mention how many teachers left his school, but I would bet the percentage was high.

Teachers want to develop expertise in their grade and subject areas. The whole attitude of not "allowing" teachers to teach their desired grade level indicates a total lack of support for teachers and their expertise. The knowledge base for teaching kindergarten is quite different than that for teaching fourth grade; teaching assignments are not interchangeable.

I met a state teacher of the year who had taught her entire career in the same room of the same school with the same grade level. She was wildly successful and a true teacher leader because she shared her expertise for this grade level with teachers around her state. The advice here to administrators is simple, "Know your teachers' skill levels and respect their career stages." A teacher who loves teaching second grade and has developed award-winning strategies for doing so should be recognized and encouraged as a leader, not forced to teach another grade.

Why do teachers leave the profession? Why does any employee leave his or her job? A commonly accepted reason for leaving any job is that the employee does not feel supported by the bosses/administrators. A second reason is that the employee does not like or get along with colleagues. All employees want to feel that their work is valued. They want to feel supported and respected. A few years ago, a news story related that over half of America's teachers held a master's degree, not just a bachelor's degree. Employees with advanced degrees have expertise and want their expertise valued.

Rinke (2014) discussed whether teaching may be a temporary occupation, not a lifelong career. In her words:

> Increased professional opportunities for women and minorities, multidimensional notions of career paths, and a proliferation of preparation routes have simultaneously impacted how new teachers view the profession, such that some beginning educators now come to the classroom with the idea of temporarily exploring teaching. (pp. 1–2)

If Rinke's proposition has merit, then administrators need to work even harder in their roles as supporters of teachers, convincing strong, competent ones to remain in the profession and grow past the survival stage.

Where do teachers go who leave their classrooms? The answers are many and varied. Some move into the business world, some into higher education, and many become school administrators.

MOVING INTO ADMINISTRATION

First and foremost, you need to ask yourself what administrative positions are open and which ones fit your interest and expertise levels. Teachers can become department chairs in large schools, guiding the work for a grade level or for a subject area in a middle or high school. This is a good choice for someone who loves his or her grade and subject and wants to still teach while doing some administrative duties for an additional stipend. Within a school, there are curriculum coordinators, assistant principals, and principals.

Moving into district administration may include getting a position as an area coordinator in special education, reading, or gifted education. Curriculum directors and personnel directors also serve at the district level, as do assistant superintendents. The job of superintendent ranks at the top of the pyramid for some aspiring administrators.

What Skills Do I Need to Move into Administration?

Obviously, before seeking an administrative position, a teacher needs to earn the right credentials. A master's degree in administration (called leadership in most states) is the minimum amount of advanced coursework required. Many states require an internship in administration before completing a program, making classroom teachers shadow administrators and complete projects with them while still teaching. Certification for the leadership position, including tests, is required.

Teachers should shop for the right graduate program that meets their needs just as they shopped for the right college as an undergraduate. Although online programs abound, some are not accepted in the state where you work, and some are much more expensive than attending a brick-and-mortar college. Check closely for the accreditation of any program you consider. Questions to ask about a graduate program include:

1. What are the total costs of tuition and fees?
2. How much work is in class, and how much is blended or online?
3. Are there cohorts of students, and do I take every class in a specific order?
4. What happens if I miss a semester because of a family issue? How do I make up that semester?
5. What are the pass rates on the state's administrative exam for students in this program?
6. Can I transfer any credits earned earlier from another institution?
7. Who teaches in this program? Will I work with full-time professors or adjuncts?
8. What are research requirements (thesis or action research)?
9. What do recent program completers say about this program?

Your program of study should include work on the following topics because they are critical for people moving into school administration:

1. Curriculum leadership: knowing what should be taught and how to meet state standards
2. Assessment: knowing how to lead teachers in assessment processes and how to interpret and share data
3. Instruction: guiding teachers to best instructional practices
4. Supervision and evaluation of teachers
5. Personnel management: hiring, induction, release of teachers
6. Professional development
7. School budgets and finance
8. Facilities management
9. School law
10. Vision and leadership skills

What Are the Advantages and Disadvantages of Moving into Leadership?

Advantages may include:

1. Increased pay
2. Doing work that affects many students, not just those in an individual classroom
3. Intrinsic satisfaction of making a difference

4. Working to improve the conditions of a school for students and teachers
5. Serving the community

Disadvantages may include:

1. Much less vacation time
2. Nights and weekends spent working
3. Less time for your family
4. Stress of being in the public eye
5. Many more responsibilities
6. A sharp learning curve for each new school year

Administrators who view their work as servant leadership take the approach that they are stewards of the schools where they work. Their long-term goal is to leave the school or program they direct in better shape than when they began their job. Strong administrators prioritize student learning and the support of their teaching faculties. They solicit and listen to feedback, valuing the expertise of the teachers and support staff with whom they work. They make the tough decisions too.

Many report that there are shortages of school administrators, and others say that the shortage is of good administrators. Either way, moving into administration is a career step for classroom teachers to consider. To find out more, start reading what administrators read: *Principal* magazine, *Principal Leadership*, and *Educational Leadership*. Go to a national conference, such as one from NAESP, the National Association of Elementary School Principals, or NASSP, the National Association of Secondary School Principals.

MOVING INTO HIGHER EDUCATION

I am often asked how I got a "cushy" job in higher education, teaching two or three classes a semester. I begin by saying that being a college professor is the hardest job that I've ever had and is actually much more difficult than teaching six high school classes a day. "What?" people respond. "That's impossible." "No," I reply. "It's a different kind of hard."

When I was a high school teacher, my job was teaching. When the lesson planning and paper grading were done, I was done. Now, teaching is only one-third of my job. When I am done with the planning and grading, I must now research and write. Those who get tenure-track positions and do not publish, even at a small private college, get fired. Really.

Additionally, I must prove that I provide service to my department, my school, my college, and my profession. I must do committee work, recruit new students on Saturdays, advise an honor society, and organize Sunday initiations for the honor society and their parents. I sit on a committee that reviews the work of my colleagues for their continued employment at the college. I sit on committees to interview and hire new faculty. One year, I led the faculty governance body, leading monthly meetings for all the college faculty and taking their issues to central administration.

I must present my research at national conferences, often paying my own airfare and lodging to do so. My college expects me to publish at least one article every year, and that article should be published in a nationally recognized, peer-reviewed journal. I received tenure after six years of doing the teaching, research, publishing, and service I have outlined. During my twelfth year at the college, I was promoted to full professor. After twenty-one years, I must still publish to earn merit raises.

Perhaps the biggest difference is office politics. I know that there are office politics everywhere—in the business world and in K–12 teaching. The difficulties of office politics of higher education seem to be magnified about 20 times from those of the public high school where I taught. Many people call the work environments of higher education a "catfish aristocracy," and that can certainly be true. (This means that people assume their professional value and worth to be well above what it really is and they make any small issue into a huge one.)

So what are the advantages to moving into higher education, and how does one do so? Time is an advantage. People who teach in colleges and universities have a different kind of workday than their K–12 counterparts. We set our office hours and can work from home. If I finish teaching at noon one day a week, I just head home. For many semesters, I have worked at home every Wednesday. It's when I do my writing and am uninterrupted. On Wednesdays, I dress in blue jeans, and my workday is from about 6:00 a.m. to 2:00 p.m. with a nice lunch break in my own kitchen. After 2:00, I can run errands or just rest.

There are many travel opportunities for college professors, and some are funded by grants. My college provides some travel money every year, with the possibility of applying for more. In my work with my professional association, I have traveled throughout the United States and to China and Africa.

College teaching is one of the few jobs where the expertise of people over sixty years of age is still respected. I know many professors who work into their seventies, and their administrators support their continued work. This is quite different than the business world.

Getting the Right Credentials for College Teaching

A doctorate is the requirement for full-time college teaching. This can mean a doctor of education degree (EdD) or a doctor of philosophy degree (PhD). I left my full-time teaching job and entered graduate school as a full-time student to earn my advanced degrees. I worked half-time for the universities, first teaching Spanish and then supervising student teachers. I had free tuition and fees by working and got the experience I needed teaching and supervising for my next job. By going to graduate school full-time, I was able to earn a master's degree in one year and a doctorate in three years, with no debt when I finished. (I should add that I have a very supportive husband.)

The route I took has become less common today because the cost of tuition has skyrocketed and few individuals feel that they can afford to quit their teaching jobs to work for very low wages as teaching assistants. Online degrees have become, and are becoming, much more acceptable. However, many colleges and universities still require an earned doctorate from a brick-and-mortar university for full-time, tenure-track professorships.

Tenure-track positions are the most sought-after ones because they are full-time positions that lead to tenure and promotions, from assistant to associate to full professor, which is the career ladder in higher education. Although all colleges and universities hire part-time and temporary instructors, these positions are not ones that pay well and may not include benefits or insurance.

When you decide to earn a doctorate, search carefully for a program that meets your needs. Special considerations include:

1. Who will serve as your advisor? Having a competent advisor is the key to finishing a dissertation in a timely manner.
2. What will be your specialty? As a former high school Spanish teacher, I had to make the decision to earn a PhD in Spanish, with a goal of becoming a professor of Spanish, or to earn the doctorate in teacher education. Becoming a teacher educator gave me many more job options, so I earned my degree in that field. Additionally, I didn't want to research Spanish linguistics or literature; I wanted to research teaching.
3. What do you want to do with your doctorate? Teach in a college? Continue to work as a school administrator? Work as an administrator or staff person in higher ed? I recently met a doctoral student who said she was spending over $50,000 to earn her doctorate. When I asked what she was going to do, she replied, "Oh, I haven't had time to think about that."
4. Consider the reputation of the university where you seek your doctorate and the success rates of its graduates in getting the kind of job you seek.
5. If you seek a job in a large research university, you need an earned doctorate from a university with a good reputation.

6. Getting a job in higher education is quite competitive. Many candidates have published articles and grants on their résumés before they finish their degrees.

Even before you earn a doctorate, read about job opportunities for professors and administrators in higher education. The Chronicle of Higher Education is a primary source for job information (https://chroniclevitae.com/job_search/new). Also, look at salaries. Experienced teachers with advanced degrees may find that jobs in higher education actually pay less than their current position. Study the advantages and disadvantages and decide what is right for you at your career stage.

KEYS FOR SUCCESS

1. Successful teachers have their own definitions of success. For some, it means staying in their classrooms, and for others it means moving into administration or higher education.
2. Successful teachers know that money is not everything. They consider personal time and lifestyle as they move through their career stages.
3. Successful teachers find support through professional organizations. They join and remain active to stay informed about teaching.
4. Successful teachers accept help throughout their careers and become leaders by helping and supporting others.
5. Successful teachers are professionals, and the most successful ones grow throughout their careers.

Chapter Twelve

Know Why They Teach

> Successful teachers know why they teach. They have a personal philosophy for their work.

I recently met an experienced teacher who had been teaching for over twenty-five years. She said she questioned her job and almost quit after her tenth year. She pondered her job over the following summer and came back to school in the fall with a new attitude. She said the difference was her self-confidence. She realized that she was teaching well and that her students were succeeding. She quit listening to naysayers and quit trying to implement every new fad. She said what so many successful teachers have said, "I shut the door to my room and the students and I learn." She found her personal philosophy and inner strength. Her students had high test scores too.

In 2012, I was invited to give a speech at an educational conference in Windhoek, Namibia, in Africa. I attended every session at the conference and learned about schools in many African nations. One teacher addressed teacher burnout in her country. She said that many young teachers left teaching because of the extreme work conditions in their schools, such as no indoor plumbing or running water. The question went through my mind, "Why would anyone teach under those circumstances?" Miraculously, many teachers do persist despite their working conditions. They certainly have developed inner strength and a philosophy to keep going every day.

I have also provided training in China for teachers and principals working in private Christian schools. These dedicated educators face myriads of challenges as they open schools, both sanctioned and nonsanctioned by their government. I have met young, dedicated teachers who start a school in their home or nearby apartment and then build a curriculum from scratch. They must raise funds, charge tuition, find faculty, and do everything needed to start a school, all while wondering if the government will close private Christian schools at some point. I marvel at the dedication of such educators, many of whom have had no formal teacher education themselves. Indeed, they have strong beliefs for what they do.

Teachers around the United States, and around the world, do indeed face challenges and stressors in their profession. Yet every day, in classrooms everywhere, teachers are succeeding. Where do teachers find their strength? What are some tried-and-true motivators? What inspires teachers who work for twenty, thirty, or even forty years in the profession?

READING ABOUT INSPIRATIONAL EDUCATORS

Many books have been written by exceptionally talented educators about how they achieved success in their classrooms. Rafe Esquith (2003), an American Teacher Award recipient, authored *There Are No Shortcuts*. The title of the epilogue to the book is "I'm Still Standing," and in that chapter, the author discussed how relationships with students have kept him motivated to teach. He wrote that "I think my next twenty years in the classroom will be even better" (p. 207).

Esquith (2003) was known for having students work with him in his classroom as early as 6:30 a.m. He was often still at school at 7:00 p.m. He traveled with students during his vacation time. After his descriptions of grueling hours and giving so much energy to the students, he wrote:

> To all of you who are proud that you put your students first, make sure you give yourself equal time. It's rather romantic to say you'd die for your students. I used to say that. I now know I'm worth more to them alive. (p. 76)

This quote makes an important point. If teachers give too much time and energy to their work, they will burn out.

Alex Kajitani (2013) authored *Owning It: Proven Strategies for Success in ALL of Your Roles as a Teacher Today*. A few of his strategies for success included having teachers share the news of what is going on in their classrooms, having teachers teach each other, putting students' needs and interests first, and doing whatever works. His advice for helping new teachers stay in the profession included "minimize negative talk," "celebrate milestones and successes," and include new hires in decision making (pp. 116–17). It is sage advice.

Donald Graves (2001) wrote an inspirational-style book for teachers titled *The Energy to Teach*. In it, he called teaching an emotional roller coaster. His research indicated that three energy drains for teachers included lack of control over time and space, lack of support (for their work), and difficult students (pp. 4–6).

Where do teachers get their energy, according to Graves (2001)? His research cited two sources—students and colleagues. He suggested listening closely to students' stories of learning for motivation. He encouraged developing strong relationships with colleagues in the school as well as with those colleagues outside of one's own school. To make those professional colleagues outside of school, consider active involvement in a professional organization and online contacts.

Noted educator Ron Clark (2015) has written unique and inspirational books about teaching, but remember that he had to start his own school to teach the way he wanted to teach. Starting one's own school is a huge challenge, even if Oprah Winfrey provides some initial funding (see also www.ronclarkacademy.com).

The list of books written by award-winning teachers and those who wrote to explain their own teaching is virtually limitless. Finding a book that inspires you can make a difference in building your own strength and fortitude to stay in the classroom. Some books inspire us but may leave us thinking "There is no way I could ever do what that teacher did." Read widely, and then sort the material you read into usable pieces. Reading and writing do help us to think through our own teaching.

ABOUT REFLECTION

I have often thought that reflection was an overused term in education. To earn certification in some states, student teachers must complete the EdTPA assessment, which forces them to explain each and every step of a lesson (http://edtpa.aacte.org). Some write forty pages of reflection about teaching one lesson, as shown in two 10-minute video clips. Teachers who embark on National Board Certification (http://www.nbpts.org/national-board-certification/) write and write to reflect on their practice. That's a lot of reflection.

Reflection can be a very valuable tool to help a teacher improve his or her teaching practice. The truth is that most of the time, the teacher must decide whether a lesson went well or bombed because administrators and colleagues are rarely in a teacher's room to provide feedback. A strong teacher knows when a lesson goes well. That perfect lesson where all students are engaged and learning makes us feel fantastic. That perfect lesson is also not usually the one the supervisor gets to see. Hence, reflection is important.

I once heard a speaker say that teachers need to "talk sense to themselves." The speaker was Chick Moorman, and his coauthored book was *Teacher Talk* (Moorman & Weber, 1989). His theory makes a lot of sense. Teachers do not give themselves enough credit for the work they do. We all need to reflect and talk to ourselves about our good work and success stories. If we make a mistake, we move on. Self-talk is reflection.

I have often joked that I taught high school classes for eight years and then went to graduate school, where I reflected on the experience. I perhaps should have reflected *during* my years of high school teaching. Now, as a college professor, I write to reflect on my teaching and the big picture of education.

30 Reflection Questions

You may want to think about these questions privately. Some may want to discuss them with a trusted colleague or mentor. Consider getting two or three teachers together and having a support group meeting that is guided by the questions. Consider writing out your answers too.

1. Think back to when you decided to become a teacher. When did you make that decision?
2. What was your real reason for becoming a teacher?
3. Is your original reason for becoming a teacher still your reason for teaching?
4. How did you become a teacher? Did you complete teacher certification as an undergraduate student or enter teaching as a career change after college?
5. Did you student-teach, or did you enter your first classroom as a provisionally certified teacher? What did you learn during student teaching?
6. What are the three most memorable events of your first year of teaching?
7. After the first year, what did you learn from your colleagues and/or administrators?
8. What kinds of professional development opportunities have you experienced in the schools/districts where you have taught?
9. Have you been a member of professional associations? If so, which ones?
10. How active have you been in a professional association, and what kinds of skills and development have you gained from that organization or any group outside of your school and district?
11. How many professional conferences have you attended in your career? How many of those conferences were national in scope?
12. Have you worked on committees in your career? If so, what did you gain from your committee work?
13. When you need a teaching idea, where do you turn for help?
14. Name the most recent book you read about teaching or education.

15. Have you completed any advanced training or degrees? How did you complete that work? Did that coursework or workshop help you to improve your teaching?
16. Are you excited when you go to work in the morning? How do you really feel each morning on a workday?
17. When someone asks you why you are a teacher, what do you say?
18. Do you consider yourself a leader in your school? If so, how are you a leader?
19. What are your career plans? How long do you see yourself teaching?
20. Do you plan to move into administration or higher education, and if so, how and when do you plan to do so?
21. Do you advise your students, your children, or others that you know to pursue teaching as a career?
22. Have you written anything about teaching? Do you keep a journal or blog?
23. Have you considered publishing something about your teaching?
24. What is the one single factor that motivates you as an educator?
25. What are your outside-of-school interests?
26. What do you do in your free time?
27. If you won the lottery tomorrow, would you continue teaching?
28. Who are the people in your school support group?
29. Who are the people in your personal support network?
30. Can you state your philosophy of education to someone in a minute? (It's called an elevator speech in the business world.)

THE REST OF MY STORY

As someone who has been a bit skeptical of reflection in the past, I am going to write out my answers to the thirty questions. Of course, a reader of this book will already know quite a few of my answers.

I decided to be a teacher in my senior year of high school. My guidance counselor was assisting me with a college application, and I told him I wanted to major in Spanish because it was my favorite subject. "Hmm," he murmured, "and what do you plan to do with a major in Spanish in our small town in central Illinois?" I didn't answer quickly, so he checked the teacher education box as a second field of study. Of course, I had heard my mother talk fondly of her short teaching career, and I thought education sounded like a good idea. In retrospect, I think I was born to teach.

My real reason for becoming a teacher was to continue to learn both Spanish and French and to earn a living doing something with them. Is this still my reason for teaching? Now, I teach people to be teachers, and I truly want to help my students start and maintain their teaching careers. Teaching is a good career and helps many people to work in their hometowns and raise families. It is a career that makes a difference in the world.

I became a teacher through a traditional route, as an undergraduate student. I completed student teaching in a middle school because my supervisor probably thought I wasn't strong enough to work in a high school. I was quiet and not that outgoing in my first field experiences. I got my first job right after graduation, at age twenty-two, in a high school in a small town. Just as the research indicates about the first year of teaching, I taught within 100 miles of my hometown, and I had to teach more of my minor than my major the first two years of teaching.

During my first year of teaching, I was surprised that not every student was as excited as I was about learning Spanish and French. I learned that students wanted As for the minimum amount of work and that homecoming was much more important than academics. I learned that students didn't know English grammar and weren't thrilled about grammar in a foreign language. I learned that students drank and used drugs. Imagine my surprise when I learned that a student kept whiskey in his locker and drank sips throughout the day.

During and after my first year of teaching, my colleagues taught me survival tactics. They taught me what the principal wanted and that there was a wide range of academic abilities among students. My colleagues taught me about the community and the power of the local school board.

The professional development offered to us was one-shot programs with outside speakers. I remember one workshop day that even had a session on "dress for success." In that session, the women learned how to tie scarves. Our professional association was a chapter of the National Education Association, and we heard speakers talk about collective bargaining and statewide educational topics.

In college, I had joined AATSP, the American Association of Teachers of Spanish and Portuguese, and its Illinois chapter. I received some mail about Saturday workshops at two neighboring universities and attended those on my own. Those workshops were very helpful because there were sessions taught by veteran foreign language teachers about teaching strategies. Finally, I found some help for teaching my subject matter!

It was through my attendance at a Saturday workshop for Spanish teachers that I received an invitation to get my master's degree. A professor at the workshop asked me why I didn't have my master's degree, and I said that teaching six classes a day kept me too busy to pursue graduate classes. He gave me a great offer when he invited me to teach Spanish at Illinois State University for one year while being a full-time graduate student. By teaching, I would have free tuition and a stipend of $4,800. (That was $4,800 a year, not a month.)

I left my job and started teaching at the college level. I knew the minute after I taught my first college class that I had found my calling. I was going to work in a college. I was convinced that I could teach Spanish at a community college and have much better working conditions than at my high school after I earned my master's degree.

Much to my surprise, there were no community college teaching jobs available when I completed my degree. I also learned that many community college instructors work for years as part-time employees before they get coveted full-time jobs. I couldn't afford to work part-time.

During my year at Illinois State University, I worked quite closely with several wonderful professors. They shared insights about the advantages of working at the university level. Two of the professors had already passed retirement age but had not retired because they simply loved their jobs too much to quit. This was an "aha" moment for me. I had gone to several retirement parties for high school teachers who had counted the days until retirement at age fifty-five and were bitter at their own parties. By contrast, these professors wanted to teach until they could no longer walk up the stairs to their classrooms. They actually said that, and their passion for their work showed. I would like to acknowledge Dr. Harriet Hutter and my German professor for being my role models at Illinois State University.

Of course, I had to earn a doctorate to get a job in higher education, so I spent three more years in graduate school to earn that degree in curriculum and instruction. During that time, I taught and supervised pre-student teachers and student teachers. I joined the Association for Supervision and Curriculum Development (ASCD) during graduate school and started reading professional articles.

It is difficult to get a tenure-track professorship immediately after graduate school, but I did get a full-time administrative/staff position after completion of my doctorate. My first job after earning my doctorate paid $6,000 more than my last year in high school teaching. I write this because the pay difference may not be much from teaching K–12 to higher education. In fact, if one earns an advanced degree while working as a K–12 administrator and then moves into higher education, there may be a pay cut.

As an administrator at Eastern Illinois University, I had a delightful job. I was sent out to schools to teach workshops for beginning teachers about how to survive and thrive in their jobs. I then developed workshops for administrators about hiring and inducting the best new teachers. I found my research area while doing this work. I have continued to research and write about the hiring, induction, and success of beginning teachers. Of course, it would have been nice to have found my true research area while earning my doctorate, but that doesn't always happen.

During my six years at Eastern Illinois University, I also joined professional networks. I joined both Phi Delta Kappa (http://pdkintl.org) and Kappa

Delta Pi (www.kdp.org). I became active in Kappa Delta Pi (KDP) by writing for its publications. My very first publication was more of a blurb than an article, but it jump-started my writing career. It appeared in the KDP *New Teacher Advocate*. When asked to sit on the national editorial committee of KDP, I finally found true professional colleagues and mentors. I served on the national KDP Board of Directors for eight years and was the international president from 2012–2014. KDP is my professional lifeline. I stay current reading its journals and online resources. I go to its annual conferences. Being connected through KDP has made a huge difference in my career.

In 1996, my husband's job took him to Atlanta, Georgia, and I needed to hunt for a job and find a position within commuting distance of Atlanta. I used my colleagues in KDP for connections and support. I found a job at Berry College, north of Atlanta, and have remained there as a teaching professor for twenty-one years as of the writing of this book.

As a teacher educator, I teach people to be teachers at all levels of K–12. I teach courses in educational psychology, curriculum, teaching methods, classroom management, and methods of teaching foreign language. I have taught supervision of instruction, curriculum theory, and models of teaching in our past graduate programs. I love the variety of courses I have been able to develop and teach as well as the teaching schedule. Each year is a bit different, and every class has unique students.

What was the last book I read about teaching? I read constantly and am currently reading Stronge and Xu's (2016) *Instructional Strategies for Effective Teaching*. When teaching at the college level, professors are supposed to update the textbooks they use frequently, and this keeps us reading many different titles.

Am I excited when I get up in the morning on workdays? Most days, yes, I am. On the first day of classes this semester, I woke up an hour before the alarm went off and got to my office a full two hours before my first class. I had butterflies in my stomach, and this was my thirty-ninth year of teaching. Butterflies are good because they indicate excitement and enthusiasm. Some days, I am not as excited. Those are the days when we have tedious meetings led by weak administrators. Office politics still bother me because we could be using those meeting times to improve issues for students and not to argue among ourselves.

When someone asks me what I do, I explain that I am a teacher educator. I teach people to be teachers. I explain that to do this I was a teacher before I became a professor and that I actually work harder now than I did as a teacher. I make a little bit more money than a teacher with my experience, but I do have some shorter days.

What are my career plans? I plan to teach another seven to eight years. I would be happy to serve as the department chair or dean if needed. I hope to speak and write during all of the remaining years in my career.

What do I do in my free time? I love to walk for exercise and to hike in beautiful settings. To celebrate my sixtieth birthday I went to Peru and hiked to Machu Picchu. Later that year, I climbed a mountain in China, north of Beijing. I came back to my job refreshed and excited. Travel is certainly an aphrodisiac for me. I also enjoy visiting my ninety-one-year-old mother and hiking on our family farm in Illinois.

If I were to win the lottery tomorrow, I would keep teaching. I would probably start skipping those negative meetings. I would give some of my winnings to needy students and donate money so that they could join professional associations as students.

What is my personal philosophy for teaching? While teaching Chinese Christian teachers, I was expected to start my classes and workshops with a prayer. I found some psalms that fit well for teaching, but I also shared a prayer that I have long used as I start my day. "Thank you, God, for this day. Thank you for my health. Thank you for the strength and patience to go out into the world and help people. Please help me to remember that helping people is service and that service is what I need to do with my life. Amen."

About thirty years ago, I was driving to speak at a conference in southern Illinois. It was one of my first big speeches about teaching. The speech was actually "A Dozen Things Successful Teachers Do." I saw a sign for a gift shop that looked interesting. I stopped, got some free coffee, and browsed. I purchased a little framed poster that became my philosophy of teaching. It reads:

> I teach because I see the hope
> An education brings,
> Because the treasures found in books
> Give children stronger wings.
> I can't replace the parents
> Of those I see each day
> But I can teach, and gently coax,
> Young hearts who come my way.
> (no author cited on the poster)

I wish each reader of this book a wonderful career in teaching—at least thirty or forty years.

KEYS FOR SUCCESS

1. Successful teachers have trained for their jobs and see the need for continual learning.
2. Successful teachers know why they teach.
3. Successful teachers reflect on their teaching.

4. Successful teachers build networks of people for personal and professional support.
5. Successful teachers may remain in their classrooms throughout their careers or move into administration or higher education. They are needed at all levels of education.
6. Successful teachers take downtime and refresh with outside-of-school activities.
7. Successful teachers evaluate their jobs and may leave for another school or district that is a better match for their skills and beliefs.
8. Successful teachers have a philosophy for their work. They have a reason to get out of bed in the morning and do the wonderful yet challenging job of teaching.

References

Armstrong, T. (2018). *Multiple intelligences in the classroom* (4th ed.). Alexandria, VA: ASCD.
Arnett, T. (2017, September 12). Why we need to change the teacher vs. tech narrative. *eSchool News: Daily Tech News & Innovation*. Retrieved from www.eschoolnews.com/2017/09/12/change-teacher-vs-tech-narrative/.
Berry, B. (2014). Going to scale with teacherpreneurs. *Phi Delta Kappan, 95*(7), 8–14.
Billingsley, B. S., Brownell, M. T., Israel, M., & Kamman, M. L. (2013). *A survival guide for new special educators*. San Francisco: Jossey-Bass.
Breaux, A., & Whitaker, T. (2010). *50 ways to improve student behavior: Simple solutions to complex challenges*. Larchmont, NY: Eye of Education.
Burgess, D. (2012). *Teach like a pirate*. San Diego, CA: Dave Burgess Consulting.
Callahan, J. F., Clark, L. H., & Kellough, R. D. (2002). *Teaching in the middle and secondary schools* (7th ed.). Upper Saddle River, NJ: Merrill Prentice Hall.
Canter, L., & Canter, M. (1993). *Succeeding with difficult students*. Santa Monica, CA: Canter.
Canter, L., & Canter, M. (2001). *Assertive discipline*. Los Angeles, CA: Canter.
Carjuzaa, J., & Kellough, R. D. (2017). *Teaching in the middle and secondary schools* (11th ed.). Boston, MA: Pearson.
Clark, R. (2015). *Move your bus: An extraordinary new approach to accelerating success in work and life*. New York, NY: Touchstone.
Clement, M. C. (2003). *But high school teaching is different! Success strategies for new secondary teachers*. Washington, DC: National Education Association.
Clement, M. C. (2011). *The mentor program kit: Step-by-step guidelines for developing a mentoring program to help new teachers succeed*. Alexandria, VA: Educational Research Service.
Clement, M. C. (2013). *Get a teaching job now*. Lanham, MD: Rowman & Littlefield.
Clement, M. C. (2017a). Helping teachers manage stress. *Communicator, 40*(5). Retrieved from www.naesp.org/communicator-january-2017/helping-teachers-manage-stress.
Clement, M. C. (2017b). Women, teaching, and stress: Five steps for coping. *The Delta Kappa Gamma Collegial Exchange, 83*(4): 39–41.
Coggins, C., & McGovern, K. (2014). Five goals for teacher leadership. *Phi Delta Kappan, 95*(7), 15–21.
Cruikshank, D. R., Bainer, D., & Metcalf, K. (1995). *The act of teaching*. New York, NY: McGraw-Hill.
Cunningham, G. (2009). *The new teacher's companion*. Alexandria, VA: ASCD.
Curtain, H., & Dahlberg, C. A. (2016). *Languages and learners: Making the match* (5th ed.). Boston, MA: Pearson.

References

DuFour, R., DuFour, R., Eaker, R., & Many, T. (2006). *Learning by doing: A handbook for professional learning communities at work*. Bloomington, IN: Solution Tree.

Dweck, C. S. (2007). *Mindset: The new psychology of success*. New York, NY: Ballantine.

Esquith, R. (2003). *There are no shortcuts*. New York, NY: Anchor Books.

Fulton, K. (June/July 2012). Upside down and inside out: Flip your classroom to improve student learning. Retrieved from https://files.eric.ed.gov/fulltext/EJ982840.pdf.

Gabriel, K. F. (2008). *Teaching unprepared students: Strategies for promoting success and retention in higher education*. Sterling, VA: Stylus.

Graves, D. H. (2001). *The energy to teach*. Portsmouth, NH: Heinemann.

Herman, K. C., & Reinke, W. M. (2015). *Stress management for teachers: A proactive guide*. New York, NY: Guilford Press.

Herrell, A., & Jordan, M. (2004). *Fifty strategies for teaching English language learners*. Upper Saddle River, NJ: Pearson.

Jacobs, H. H. (2010). Upgrading the curriculum. In H. H. Hayes (Ed.), *Curriculum 21: Essential education for a changing world*. Alexandria, VA: ASCD.

Jones, M. (2016). *Life's a marathon*. Austin, TX: Matt Jones International.

Kajitani, A. (2013). *Owning it: Proven strategies for success in all of your roles as a teacher today* (2nd ed.). San Bernardino, CA: Kajitani Education.

Kronowitz, E. L. (2008). *The teacher's guide to success*. Boston, MA: Pearson.

Loewus, L. (2017, August 15). The nation's teaching force is still mostly white and female. https://www.edweek.org/ew/articles/2017/08/15/the-nations-teaching-force-is-still-mostly.html.

Martin, C. C., & Hauth, C. (2015). *The survival guide for special education teachers* (2nd ed.). Arlington, VA: Council for Exceptional Children.

Marzano, R. J., Pickering, D. J., & Pollock, J. E. (2001). *Classroom instruction that works: Research-based strategies for increasing student achievement*. Alexandria, VA: ASCD.

Mazzone, M. N., & Miglionico, B. J. (2014). *Stress-busting strategies for teachers: How do I manage the pressures of teaching?* Alexandria, VA: ASCD Arias.

Minkel, J. (2017). Four things to visualize as you set up your classroom for the first day of school. Retrieved from www.edweek.org/tm/articles/2017/08/16/four-things-to-visualize-as-you-set.html?cmp=eml-enl-tu-news2&print=1.

Moorman, C., and Weber, N. (1989). *Teacher talk*. Merrill, MI: Authors.

Nieto, S. (2013). *Finding joy in teaching students of diverse backgrounds*. Portsmouth, NH: Heinemann.

Palmer, P. (1998). *The courage to teach*. San Francisco, CA: Jossey-Bass.

Popham, W. J. (2011). *Classroom assessment: What teachers need to know* (6th ed.). Boston, MA: Pearson.

Responsive Classroom. (2015). *The first six weeks of school* (2nd ed.). Turner Falls, MA: Responsive Classroom.

Rinke, C. R. (2014). *Why half of teachers leave the classroom: Understanding recruitment and retention in today's schools*. Lanham, MD: Rowman & Littlefield.

Silver, H. F., Strong, R. W., & Perini, M. J. (2007). *The strategic teacher: Selecting the right research-based strategy for every lesson*. Upper Saddle River, NJ: Pearson.

Smith, D., Frey, N., Pumpian, I., & Fisher, D. (2017). *Building equity: Policies and practices to empower all learners*. Alexandria, VA: ASCD.

Spencer, E. J. (2016). Professional learning communities: Keeping the focus on instructional practice. *Kappa Delta Pi Record, 52*(2), 83–85.

Steffy, B. E., Wolfe, M. P., Pasch, S. H., & Enz, B. J. (2000). *Life cycle of the career teacher*. Thousand Oaks, CA: Corwin.

Stronge, J. H., Grant, L. W., & Xu, X. (2017). *Designing effective assessments*. Bloomington, IN: Solution Tree.

Stronge, J. H., & Xu, X. (2016). *Instructional strategies for effective teaching*. Bloomington, IN: Solution Tree.

Stufft, C. J., Abrams, S. S., & Gerber, H. R. (2016). Critical thinking and layered understandings: Book clubs, videogames, and adolescent learning. Retrieved from www.alan-ya.org/wp-content/uploads/2014/11/m96-102-ALAN-Sum161.pdf.

Walsh, J. A., & Sattes, B. D. (2015). *Questioning for classroom discussion*. Alexandria, VA: ASCD.
Wiggins, G., & McTighe, J. (2000). *Understanding by design*. Upper Saddle River, NJ: Pearson.
Wong, H. K., & Wong, R. T. (2009). *The first days of school: How to be an effective teacher*. Mountain View, CA: Harry K. Wong.
Woolfolk, A. (2016). *Educational psychology* (13th ed.). Boston, MA: Pearson.

Index

advance organizers, 111
assess prior interest and knowledge (APIK), 60
applied behavioral analysis (ABA), 41
assessment, vocabulary of, 85

brain-based learning, 15

career stages, 149
certification, 2
classroom management: assertive discipline, 36; procedures, 35; rules and consequences, 36
Common Core State Standards, 48
concept attainment, 63
cooperative learning, 68
curriculum mapping, 56

discussions, 66–67

essential questions, 54
evaluation of teachers, 124

Family Educational Rights and Privacy Act (FERPA), 131
flipped classroom, 77

Gardner, Howard, 20
gifted students, support for, 109
grading systems, 93; total point, 94
group work, 67–68

induction, 142
interest inventories, 34, 60
interviews, 5

leadership, teacher, 147, 148
lectures, 61–62
lesson planning, 50; four-step plan, 51
licensure, 2

master's degree, 3
modeling, 64
motivation, 24

Nieto, Sonia, 103

parent communication: conferences, 118; e-mail, 117; phone calls, 117; text messages, 117
professional associations, 4; Kappa Delta Pi honor society, 136, 141, 144, 163
professional dress, 33
professional learning communities (PLCs), 137, 145
PTA/PTO, 126

questioning, 64–65

rubric, 88
resume, 5

technology, uses of, 75; classroom blog, 75; gaming, 80
test writing : guidelines, 90; kinds of test questions, 91
think, pair, share, 62
time management, 129

understand by design, 49

Vygotsky, Lev, 19

Wong, Harry K., 29

Zone of Proximal Development (ZPD), 19

About the Author

Mary C. Clement has researched the hiring and induction of teachers for over twenty years, and her work has resulted in thirteen previous books and a hundred and forty articles. She has presented her work at ASCD and NAESP conferences as well as for Phi Delta Kappa and Kappa Delta Pi. In 2013, she received the STAR award from the American Association for Employment in Education (AAEE) for her contribution to the research on teacher hiring.

A former high school teacher, she directed the Beginning Teacher Program at Eastern Illinois University for six years, providing training to administrators on how to induct and retain new teachers. Clement is now a professor of teacher education at Berry College in north Georgia. She earned her doctorate from the University of Illinois at Urbana-Champaign.

www.ingramcontent.com/pod-product-compliance
Lightning Source LLC
Chambersburg PA
CBHW030113010526
44116CB00005B/224